Getting **Familiar** with the **Unfamiliar** 3

Understanding Unfamiliar Text Through Close Reading: NCEA Level Three

Kathryn **Fitzgerald** and **Tania** Roxborogh

NELSON
A Cengage Company

Getting Familiar with the Unfamiliar 3
1st Edition
Kathryn Fitzgerald
Tania Roxborogh

Cover designer: Cheryl Smith, Macarn Design
Text designer: Cheryl Smith, Macarn Design
Production controller: Siew Han Ong

Any URLs contained in this publication were checked for currency during the production process. Note, however, that the publisher cannot vouch for the ongoing currency of URLs.

Acknowledgements

The authors and publisher wish to thank the following people and organisations for permissions to use the following resources in this workbook.

Page 7, *Philosophy from a kayak on a summer's evening* courtesy of Grant Shimmin and Stuff. Page 17, *Ferry Road* by Mary McCallum courtesy of Submarine Press. Page 29, *The Wrong One* courtesy of Chiao Lin. Page 36, *Mother* courtesy of Renee Liang. Page 44, *The Absolute Book* by Elizabeth Knox courtesy of Victoria University Press, Wellington. Page 46, *Fairy Tale* courtesy of Fiona Farrell. Page 49, *How We Fell* courtesy of Glen Colquhoun. Page 58, *Near Death Experience* courtesy of John Allison. Page 70, *The Writing Teacher* courtesy of T.K. Roxborogh. Page 77, *My Father Today* courtesy of Sam Hunt. Page 84, *From Double Take* courtesy of Emma Neale. Page 87, *For Andrew* by Fleur Adcock courtesy of Victoria University Press, Wellington. Page 90, *Whakam* courtesy of Kirsty Dunn. Page 102, *Feelings and Memories of a Kuia* courtesy of Apirana Taylor. Page 114 *Is it hot enough for you yet?* courtesy of David Slack and Stuff. Page 121, *Me, the Labourer* courtesy of Eti Sa'aga. Page 128, *Myself, Looking Back* courtesy of Grahame Sydney and Craig Potton Publishing. Page 130, *It's taken me all morning for her to do this* courtesy of Nicole Easthope and The Cuba Press.

Author acknowledgments

I want to thank Tania for choosing me to work on this project with; it's been interesting, challenging and educational. Tania's continual manaaki, friendship and perspective has been invaluable. I also want to thank my mum for minding my then newborn son so I could write Book 1 of this series. Finally, my deepest gratitude goes to my husband, Liam, for supporting me from the start. We started this project as a newly married couple and we are now the proud parents of two young children so there is no way I could have done it without him.
Kathryn

I want to thank Kathryn for once again being a fantastic co-author, teacher, writer, and much respected friend. Ka aroha ki a koe.
Tania

For product information and technology assistance,
in Australia call **1300 790 853**;
in New Zealand call **0800 449 725**

For permission to use material from this text or product, please email
aust.permissions@cengage.com

National Library of New Zealand Cataloguing-in-Publication Data
A catalogue record for this book is available from the National Library of New Zealand.

978 0 17 0454 445

Cengage Learning Australia
Level 7, 80 Dorcas Street
South Melbourne, Victoria Australia 3205

Cengage Learning New Zealand
Unit 4B Rosedale Office Park
331 Rosedale Road, Albany, North Shore 0632, NZ

For learning solutions, visit **cengage.co.nz**

Printed in China by 1010 Printing International Limited.
3 4 5 6 7 24 23

Contents

INTRODUCTION FOR TEACHERS

The aim of this book is to provide for students who have been working their way through the series. It is a final 'step' in their learning strategies to read and understand texts. Specifically, it has a focus on the current structure of the NCEA L3 external examination. It is intended for students (and teachers) wishing to develop their understanding of how to critically analyse texts in preparation for assessment. Using the tasks as a model, teachers will be able to create their own resources to help students continue to develop a critical eye when they read a range of English texts. Many of the tasks are repeated in the sections to allow teachers to work through the book as suits their needs/the needs of the students.

INTRODUCTION FOR STUDENTS

"Hutia te rito o te harakeke
Kei whea to kōmako e kō?
Ki mai ki ahau
He aha te mea nui o te ao?
Maku e kō atu,
he tāngata, he tāngata, he tāngata ..."

If the heart of the harakeke was removed,
where would the bellbird sing?
If I was asked what was the most important
thing in the world
I would be compelled to reply,
it is people, it is people, it is people.

These words were spoken by Te Aupouri rangatira, Mere Ngaroto. She'd just learned that some of her relatives were planning to kill a group of visitors to her marae at Ohaki. Rather than just saying 'Kaua e mate rātou/Don't kill them', she employs imagery, referring to an important object all her listeners would be familiar with, harakeke – flax. She does not need to 'explain' this in her exhortation – with a bit of consideration, they would see the connection, understand the allusions and connotations as they relate to her purpose: make her relatives see that all things are connected – they, to the visitors; the visitors, to their ancestors; their ancestors, to themselves. To hurt these manuhiri is to hurt the wider whānau group – both living and dead. The pa harakeke/flax bush becomes a metaphor for a healthy family. By the way, Mere was successful and the lives of the visitors were spared.

This idea of whakapapa (connection, relationships) is useful in making sense of texts we are not familiar with. So:

- look for the connections – both inside and outside the text
- look for the literary and figurative meanings
- consider the reasons why particular words, phrases and imagery have been used.

In the same way a mechanic will choose to use a wrench to unscrew a bolt rather than pliers, a writer will use the *best* technique to suit their purpose. If you aren't, get familiar with the tools used by writers to communicate their messages. This workbook is designed to help you do that.

For examination answers, markers are looking for concise responses to the question which concentrates on only a few of the aspects but discusses them in depth, creating a holistic, rather than a 'list of techniques' approach. For Merit and Excellence, you are expected to discuss this analysis of 'how and why' the writer constructed the text this way. In other words, providing in-depth discussion and unpacking of the effect of aspects and linking back to the author's purpose.

     ISBN: 978017045445

ChapterOne: PLACES

SET 1

PROSE: *Philosophy from a kayak on a summer's evening* by Grant Shimmin

Pre-reading activities

Before beginning any analysis of a text, it is a good idea to complete some pre-reading activities. Pre-reading activities are designed to kick-start your brain, allowing you to reach into it and consider things you know but that you may have forgotten about. Activating your brain before reading a text you've never seen before helps you understand the text in more detail from the first reading.

1 PREDICTING

The title of any text is important. It is often a metaphor for the overall purpose of the text but sometimes can be taken literally. Often it is chosen with care, to give a hint of what is to come without giving the game away. A trick can be to read the title alongside the last two or three lines of a prose piece as often this summarises the overall intention/purpose/ideas of the piece; but more on this later (when we have read the piece!).

The title of this piece is *Philosophy from a kayak on a summer's evening* and is by Grant Shimmin.

First of all, let's remind you what philosophy means:

> Philosophy is the study or creation of theories about basic things such as the nature of existence, knowledge, and thought, or about how people should live.

Definition from collinsdictionary.com

Now, let's break down that title.

a What emotions/feelings/images does this title evoke (*to cause to occur*) for you? Use the space below to jot down your ideas; you could even draw them if you like.

ISBN: 978017045445

b What expectations do you have for this piece considering this title? That is, will it be a serious tone or more playful? Consider the following publication details:

Grant Shimmin; January 11 2020; Stuff.co.nz; opinion section.

_____

_____

_____

_____

2 VOCABULARY WORK

One of the most daunting things about reading any new (unfamiliar) text is that it might include words that you don't understand. Usually the best thing to do is to reread the sentence or read on a sentence or two. Using your own prior knowledge, you can often discern (*to see or recognise by sight, some other sense or intellect*) the meaning.

a In this text, we have chosen 8 words/phrases that you may not be familiar with. Draw a line between the word and its correct definition. Check your answers in the back when you have finished.

WORD	DEFINITION
obscured	Pertaining to the sky or visible heaven.
celestial	Pretending to have a particular opinion or attitude.
sparse	Te reo Māori word for work.
rendezvous	Not clear or plain; ambiguous, vague, or uncertain.
postured politicians	To meet up with someone, often secretly.
vested	Fixed; settled; absolute.
Stoicism	Small in number or amount and spread out over an area.
mahi	Philosophy which teaches self-control when faced with hardship.

Definitions from collinsdictionary.com

b Write three sentences that include a word(s) from above to prove your understanding. Challenge yourself to include two of the vocabulary words per sentence. Underline the words you have chosen.

i _____

_____

ii _____

_____

iii _____

_____

Reading the text

Read the text through once, taking your time, and out loud if possible. Underline or circle any words you are unsure of or words which 'catch your eye'. Perhaps put a question mark (?) next to anything you do not understand.

Philosophy from a kayak on a summer's evening

As we drove, I wondered if it was going to be a wasted journey.

It had been still when we set out from the central city, even if not especially warm, but the cloud was building up and at times the sun was obscured as we headed for the hills. It was having a direct impact on my enthusiasm for a venture I'd proposed. But we'd started out, we might as well continue.

As we rounded the bend that offered the last sweeping view of Cass Bay before the road descended, my spirits were raised. The water was calm and inviting. (...)

About 100 metres offshore, I glanced to my right and the sun, peeking from beneath thickish cloud as it descended towards the ridge line crowning the Port Hills, was fanning rays out across the water like some sort of celestial royal flush. Almost as though it was telling me my gamble in heading out had paid off.

In fact, that was just the start of the payout. I headed round to Corsair Bay, riding a gentle swell and catching occasional glances back at the sun. It had broken free of its cloudy moorings and was putting on a show for the sparse late evening crowd of myself and the occasional walker on the track above the harbour.

It had one other member, the friend who'd accompanied me and was now having a dip off one of Cass Bay's small secluded beaches.

As I headed back to rendezvous with him, I found myself stopping occasionally, drifting in the warm evening sunshine, listening to the birdsong from the hillside above. It was something like peace, contentment even, which suddenly seemed extraordinary.

It wasn't lost on me that less than a week earlier, on New Year's Day, I'd been out on this bay in even calmer conditions, but with the eerie accompaniment of Australian bushfire smoke that obliterated the evening sun and made the whole scene seem like a series of old sepia tone images.

That those fires raged on across the Tasman, with thousands fighting for their homes and their lives, while politicians postured and vested fossil fuel interests fouled the air further with the stench of bulls..t, seemed a lot more than 2000km away just then.

It was hard to think, too, of the unfolding situation in the Middle East, where America's assassination of Iranian general Qassem Soleimani, authorised by Donald Trump, had brought the reprisal, just hours earlier, of an Iranian missile strike on a US base in Iraq. What might happen next? (...)

Despite the optimism that had greeted the dawn of the 2020s, I had been seeing more and more people bemoaning the way the new year had kicked off. Depending on the version you prefer, the world was either going to hell in a handcart or a hand basket.

It was tough not to feel down about the future of the human race. (...)

But at that moment, on the haven of our stunning harbour, I was reminded that the onslaught of negativity and hopelessness isn't all there is. There is still kindness in the world, compassion, empathy, from many ordinary people, who do what they can where they are and make life better for others, maybe a few, maybe many, but they persist, shining through the gaps in the global gloom cloud.

David Slack, column-writing gem that he is, had reminded us days earlier of the philosophy of Stoicism, through the words of a courageous newspaper publisher friend:

'Concentrate on what is within your power to do ... disregard the hysteria and wrongness around you. Preoccupy yourself with doing what is in your power to be done.'

It doesn't mean being unaware of what's going on in the world. It's simply an acknowledgement of one's inability to change that.

I've been lucky enough to get to know the founders of the thriving national charity Good Bitches Baking over the last couple of years. It started as a small-scale attempt to give struggling people a boost through baking, now it has some 2300 bakers doing the mahi nationally. (...)

If only each of us, ordinary people, had a vision of what is in our power to do, for one person, a handful, thousands. I think it could help bring genuine perspective to living in a world gone mad. That and drifting on a harbour where the sun is turning the water to molten gold.

Grant Shimmin

Immediate response

1   Use the space below to record your first impressions. You can jot down singular words, phrases and/or ideas.

2   What aspect of the text did you most engage with? What will you remember?

_____

_____

_____

_____

3   What does it make *you* think about?

_____

_____

_____

_____

4   How would a second reading be different? What would you focus on the next time you read the piece?

_____

_____

_____

_____

5   How would different people view this text differently (dependent on gender, age, ethnic background, worldview, etc.)?

_____

_____

_____

_____

_____

_____

Post-reading questions

Read the text again.

1 What picture of the world, and our place in it, is Shimmin building in this piece? Write your answer in full sentences. Bonus points if you include a quote(s) to back up your points.

_____

_____

_____

_____

_____

2 Why do you think Shimmin was thinking about these things while out kayaking?

_____

_____

_____

_____

Unpacking the text

1 THE TITLE UNLOCKED

The title of a text will have a figurative and a literal meaning. The literal meaning will tell you about the **subject** of the text and the figurative meaning will tell you about the **theme** and/or **purpose** of the text.

You have already considered the words in the title. Now we want you to think about the possible meanings in light of what you now know.

a Look closely again at each word and consider the title.

Literal meaning		Figurative meaning
	'Philosophy from a kayak on a summer's evening'	

b Complete the following.

Philosophy from a kayak on a summer's evening means [literal meaning] _____

_____ and also means [figurative meaning]

_____.

This is an appropriate title for the text because _____

_____.

Remember when we mentioned on page 5 that a trick can be to read the title alongside the last two or three lines of a prose piece as often this summarises the overall intention/purpose/ideas of the piece?

Well, let's delve (*to dive deeper, discover new information by searching*) into that now.

> **Philosophy from a kayak on a summer's evening** *If only each of us, ordinary people, had a vision of what is in our power to do, for one person, a handful, thousands. I think it could help bring genuine perspective to living in a world gone mad. That and drifting on a harbour where the sun is turning the water to molten gold.*

c   So, what do you think is the author's purpose in writing this piece?

_____

_____

_____

_____

2   IDENTIFYING THE TONE

> Tone, in written composition, is an attitude of a writer towards a subject or an audience. Tone is generally conveyed through the choice of words, or the viewpoint of a writer on a particular subject. Every written piece covers a central theme or subject matter. The manner in which a writer approaches this theme and subject is the tone. The tone can be formal, informal, serious, comic, sarcastic, sad, or cheerful, or it may be any other existing attitude.

Source: https://literarydevices.net/tone/

a   What types of feelings and atmosphere does this piece create for you?

_____

_____

_____

b   Reread the text and:
  i   Highlight, using differing colours, positive and negative words and phrases.
  ii Organise the positive and negative words and phrases into two lists. We have started this for you.

Positive	Negative
raised	wasted
calm	direct impact
inviting	obscured

iii Look at the words listed above. Describe the tone of the passage. Do not use the words 'positive' or 'negative'. Be more specific, e.g. 'resentful', 'hopeful', 'nervous', 'funny'.

The tone is mostly _____ because of words such as _____

_____.

c Identify the main subject/topic of the text.

_____

d Write down a quote that describes (or shows) the subject.

_____

_____

e Describe the writer's attitude to the subject. Use examples from the text to support your answer.

The writer is _____ because

he uses words like _____ when describing

_____.

These words make the reader think about _____

_____ because _____

_____

_____

_____

3 FIND THE PATTERN

A writer selects the order, pace, and manner in which information is communicated to the reader. They do this because they want us to 'read' their work in a particular way. Identifying the structure of a text adds to our understanding of the purpose. Often this is recognised as a pattern.

Looking at the individual pattern pieces is part of what we call unpacking the text and is a key skill in being able to critically analyse. For this text, we will look at the pattern of tone.

a Looking at your coloured highlights of positive and negative words and phrases from question **2b** how would you describe the pattern?

_____

_____

_____

b After seeing the pattern, what is it that the writer wants us to learn/know/understand about our place in the world? Why do you think he believes it is important that we know this? You can use our sentence starters or write your own on a separate piece of paper and attach to this page. 📎

The writer wants us to understand that _____

because _____

_____

It's important we understand this/his truth so that/because _____

_____

_____

Identifying and discussing the effects of how the article is communicated

We have deliberately waited until near the end of your analysis to get you to identify techniques. This is because it is crucial that you **understand the ideas** in the passage in detail prior to understanding **how** they are communicated.

Identifying the **subject** and **tone** of the passage like you did in the earlier activities helps you understand the writer's purpose. This purpose is then communicated through a variety of **language features** or **language techniques**. These terms are used interchangeably in this book.

1 Complete the following grid of **language features/techniques**. We have done some of it for you and provided space for you to add one of your own. You could continue this grid on your own paper and attach here. 📎

Technique	Example(s)	Effect	Why it is effective	How does this develop our understanding of the writer's purpose?
Imagery	'the cloud was building up and at times the sun was obscured …'		Because it transports us to the moment with Shimmin; even if we haven't kayaked before, we can clearly imagine this scene – basically happening anywhere in New Zealand.	
Proper noun	'New Year's Day' 'Tasman' 'Donald Trump' 'Qassem' 'Soleimani'	Makes everything feel more real – a complete break from the beautiful imagery created earlier about kayaking on calm water in a sunset.		
Alliteration	'**f**ossil **f**uel interests **f**ouled the air **f**urther' '**g**aps in the **g**lobal **g**loom cloud'			It hammers home the negative points of Shimmin's text and really makes them stand out. We are aware that within this lovely musing, he does make some valid points.
Fact	'2000km away' 'Iranian missile strike on a US base' '2300 bakers'			

Language focus: Passive/active voice

An aspect of tone is 'voice' – specifically writing in the active or passive voice. We look at the arrangement of the words in the sentence: the subject, the verb, the object.

In the **active voice**, the subject (or the actor) comes before the verb (action). This makes the tone of the sentence direct, dynamic, energetic. The subject is the focus of the sentence.

In contrast, the **passive voice** positions the subject (actor) at or towards the end of the sentence thus putting the focus on either the verb (action) or the object (the thing which is being affected).

For example, Shimmin's article is written in both the active voice and the passive voice. This is appropriate because in some parts, the focus of the piece is people and what they are doing whereas in other parts, description of the place seems to be more important as it mimics the way in which what he sees provokes contemplation of ideas in the author.

Here's one example of active voice: *'I headed round to Corsair Bay, riding a gentle swell …'*. In the example, *I headed round* is the element Shimmin wants you to see first: what the kayakers are doing, how and where he is doing it is secondary.

If, on the other hand, the author's focus was on the place, he might write in the passive voice such as: *'Riding a gentle swell and catching occasional glances back at the sun, I headed round to Corsair Bay, …'*. The effect of this is to 'promote' the importance of how the action is done and the place regardless of who is doing the action.

Here's an example of passive voice: *'As we drove, I wondered if it was going to be a wasted journey.'* The act of driving is at the start of the sentence adding weight to the idea that something like long car rides helps one work through thoughts.

Note the change in tone and focus if we were to rewrite this in the active voice: *'I wondered if it was going to be a wasted journey as we drove.'* The subject (actor) 'I' is at the start and is therefore the most important element of the sentence; the verb 'wondered' comes second and continues to keep the focus of what the subject (actor) is doing; where and when come later.

1   Identify the subject (actor) of each sentence from the Shimmin article on page 7 and identify whether the example is in the passive or active voice.

   a   As I headed back to rendezvous with him, I found myself stopping occasionally …

   _____

   b   The water was calm and inviting.

   _____

   c   As we rounded the bend that offered the last sweeping view of Cass Bay before the road descended, my spirits were raised.

   _____

   d   David Slack, column-writing gem that he is, had reminded us days earlier …

   _____

2   Now rewrite these sentences, changing the voice from passive to active or active to passive. You will need to alter/change some of the words to ensure the sentence is grammatically correct. We've done the first one for you.

   a   *I found myself stopping occasionally as I headed back to rendezvous with him.* _____

   b   _____

   c   _____

   d   _____

Putting it together

QUESTION ONE

Discuss the way in which the writer explores how people can have an impact on the world, referring to at least TWO specific aspects of written text.

Aspects may include imagery, proper nouns, alliteration, facts, repetition, allusion.

Let's first take a moment to understand what it is the question is asking you to do. It is useful to annotate the question to remind yourself to address each aspect in your answer. We have done this for you this time.

> Means specific techniques/aspects used, including structure/tone/word choice.

> This is 'the what' you need to talk about.

Discuss the way in which the writer explores how people can have an impact on the world, referring to at least TWO specific aspects of written text.

> This means you must provide specific, accurate, relevant points – with examples and explanation of the aspects as they relate to our place in the world.

You should start your answer using the words of the question.

If you are stuck, you can use some of the sentence starters below to help you:

- *The writer wants to tell us about what negative things people are doing because …*
- *He uses the techniques of … [name technique and include the example] which has the effect of …*
- *The writer also wants to tell us about the positive things people are doing because …*
- *The technique of … [name technique and include the example] has the effect of …*
- *His attitude towards society/people is …*
- *We see this when he says …*
- *The writer uses [insert name of aspect] when he says [insert quote] to show …*
- *Another technique he uses here is …*
- *The effect of this/these aspect(s) …*
- *A third aspect used to explore the [insert specific description of a positive example] is [insert aspect] evidenced in this example [quote], which means …*
- *The reason for this is …*
- *This highlights … because …*
- *The writer wants us to consider … because …*

  　ISBN: 9780170454445

ISBN: 9780170454445

POEM: *Ferry Road* by Mary McCallum

Pre-reading activities

The same as with a prose piece, before beginning any analysis of poetry, it is a good idea to complete some pre-reading activities. Pre-reading activities are designed to kick-start your brain, allowing you to reach into it and consider things you know that you may have forgotten about.

1 PREDICTING

a We have a pretty straightforward title here: *Ferry Road*. Use the box below to break down what each word could mean.

Ferry	Road

b From your musings (*thoughts, ponderings, reflections*), what do you think is the subject matter of the text?

_____

_____

c Another good pre-reading activity to engage your brain is to make some predictions from a selection of phrases from the poem:

> **Quoting explained**
> **...** indicates that this is not the start or end of a sentence but words not relevant at this stage have been omitted.
> **/** indicates a line break in the poetry.

  i 'We walk it to get to the bush' – what do you think 'it' is?

_____

_____

  ii '... and how fast we walk / to be ahead ...' – what do you think the narrator wants to 'be ahead' of?

_____

_____

  iii '... splashes of rātā,' – what is rātā? How does this give us a clue as to what country this poem is set in?

_____

_____

  iv '... people / disembarking furious with / hope ...' – why is this an oxymoron?

_____

_____

  v Look at your musings from question **b** after breaking down the title. How do these change now you have looked at four quotes from the poem?

_____

_____

_____

_____

Reading the text

Read the poem, out loud if possible. And then read it again making any annotations that come instinctively to you: question marks, words/images which stand out, etc.

Ferry Road

We walk it to get to the bush
and all the way up watch
the weather coming in

from the heads – and by weather
5   I mean a line of something
where there was nothing –

turn and turn again to see
it drawn and redrawn
on the water, closer each

10   time, and how fast we walk
to be ahead, to the top
of the road and on to the track

for the ridge, past the newly
growing spindly things, knitted
15   cobwebs, splashes of rātā, up

into the sack of green, confetti
of beech leaves –
Hilly, that's her name, up ahead
and me and the dog at the back –
20   and then we stop at the blasted tree
and look down. All the weather,

that harbour, the water crinkled
as if smiling, the wharf—hand
out and greeting—the bay and

25   the jostle of houses, the point
where the pā of Te Hiha once
stood, watching over water,

weather and ships, people
disembarking furious with
30   hope. Today not a single

boat, not even a ferry. Still we
climb, minds on each fast footfall, the celebration of leaves,

air quick now with weather,
35   the way we three breathe
and breathe and breathe.

Mary McCallum

Immediate response

1 Use the space below to record your first impressions. You can jot down singular words, phrases and/or ideas.

```




```

2 What aspect of the text did you most engage with? What will you remember?

_____

_____

_____

3 What does it make *you* think about?

_____

_____

_____

4 How would different people view this poem differently (dependent on gender, age, ethnic background, worldview, etc.)?

_____

_____

_____

Unpacking the text

1 IDENTIFYING THE TONE

> Tone, in written composition, is an attitude of a writer towards a subject or an audience. Tone is generally conveyed through the choice of words, or the viewpoint of a writer on a particular subject. Every written piece covers a central theme or subject matter. The manner in which a writer approaches this theme and subject is the tone. The tone can be formal, informal, serious, comic, sarcastic, sad, or cheerful, or it may be any other existing attitude.

Source: https://literarydevices.net/tone/

a What types of feelings and atmosphere does this piece create for you?

_____

_____

_____

b Reread the text and:

   i Highlight, using differing colours, positive and negative words and phrases.

   ii Organise the positive and negative words and phrases into two lists.

Positive	Negative

   iii Look at the words listed above. Describe the tone of the poem. Do not use the words 'positive' or 'negative'. Be more specific, e.g. 'resentful', 'hopeful', 'nervous', 'funny'.

The tone is mostly _____ because of words such as _____

_____

_____.

c Identify the main subject/topic of the poem.

_____

d Write down a quote that describes (or shows) the subject.

_____

_____

e Describe the writer's attitude to the subject. Use examples from the poem to support your answer.

The writer is _____ because

she uses words like _____ when describing

_____.

These words make the reader think about _____

_____ because _____

_____.

Summarise

1 In no more than two sentences, write what this poem is about.

_____

_____

_____

2 Complete the following sentence. You should include a description of what the poet wants us to learn/know/ understand about our world/about life and why we need to learn this.

The poet wanted to teach us about _____

_____ because _____

_____.

Identifying the 'point of change'

All fiction (poetry and narrative prose) has a 'point of change' in it. The point of change shows us the writer's **attitude** towards the subject, which helps us understand the writer's purpose. Identifying and understanding the point of change is a strategy used to analyse the poem.

1 Identify the line where the point of change occurs. _____

2 Describe the atmosphere before this change. _____

_____

_____

3 Identify two words that contribute to this atmosphere.

a _____ **b** _____

4 Describe what the atmosphere is after the change.

_____

_____

Identifying and discussing the effects of how the poem is communicated

Identifying the **tone** and **point of change** of the poem like you did in the earlier activities helps you understand the poet's purpose. This purpose is then communicated through a variety of **language features** or **language techniques**. These terms are used interchangeably in this book.

1 The following **language features/techniques** can be found in the poem. Find and label on the text (on page 17) an example of each of the techniques in the box below. Refer to the glossary (at the back of the book) if you do not know these words.

alliteration	dash	repetition
use of te reo Māori	personification	oxymoron

2 Complete the following grid of **language features/techniques**. We have done some of it for you and provided space for you to add one of your own. You could continue this grid on your own paper and attach here.

Technique	Example(s)	Effect	Why it is effective	How does this develop our understanding of the writer's purpose?
Dash	'... the wharf—hand / out and greeting— the bay ...'			

 ISBN: 9780170454445

Technique	Example(s)	Effect	Why it is effective	How does this develop our understanding of the writer's purpose?
Repetition	'drawn and redrawn' 'breathe / and breathe and breathe'		Because it is a simple act that we all do and are familiar with.	
Use of te reo Māori	'splashes of rātā'	Lets us know the poem is set in New Zealand.		
Personification	'the jostle of houses'			It links to the idea that although 'we three' are the only ones out, they are not the only ones there.

Language focus: Rhythm

When reading poetry, try to see the poem as a piece of music. The poet has constructed the poem to be read in a very specific way and will use a range of techniques to ensure that the correct rhythm is experienced.

For example, the follow techniques are commonly used to contribute to the rhythm (or beat) of a poem:

- the use of punctuation
- line spaces
- run-on lines
- alliteration
- vowel sounds
- short and long words (single- and multiple-syllable words)
- words grouped together
- the stress on a particular word (or parts of words) in a line.

The shorter the words and lines and fewer punctuation marks, the 'faster' the rhythm. In contrast, longer words, longer lines, clusters of words, more punctuation, longer vowels, all 'slow' the rhythm.

> McCallum says of this poem:
> 'I was conscious when writing the poem that the rhythm and syntax **should evoke the business of walking up a hill as much as the language does**.'

1 The poem starts with short one-syllable words (mostly with hard consonant sounds). Give an example which shows this and explain the effect.

_____

_____

2 There is deliberate alliteration. Find an example from the poem which shows the people in the poem are speeding up.

_____

_____

3 What is the effect of the one long sentence (lines 1–21) as they climb?

_____

_____

_____

4 After the one long walking sentence, the next sentence is essentially a long list of nouns/things. Discuss the connection between this list and the action in the poem.

_____

_____

_____

5 McCallum uses dashes around 'hand / out and greeting'. She says this is to make this physically like the wharf, hand out. What is the effect of this punctuation on our impression of the wharf?

_____

_____

_____

Putting it together

QUESTION TWO

Discuss the way in which the writer explores her response to the surroundings, referring to at least TWO specific aspects of written text.

Aspects may include repetition, use of te reo Māori, personification, syntax.

Let's first take a moment to understand what it is the question is asking you to do. It is useful to annotate the question to remind yourself to address each aspect in your answer. We have done this for you this time.

> Means specific techniques/aspects used, including structure/tone/word choice.

> This is 'the what' you need to talk about.

Discuss the way in which the writer explores her response to the surroundings, referring to at least TWO specific aspects of written text.

> This means you must provide specific, accurate, relevant points – with examples and explanation of the aspects as they relate to her response to the surroundings.

You should start your answer using the words of the question.

If you are stuck, you can use some of the sentence starters below to help you:

- *The writer notices [insert examples] because …*
- *The writer takes us through the journey of their walk because …*
- *The poet's attitude towards the other person is …*
- *The writer uses [insert name of aspect] when she says [insert quote] to show …*
- *Another technique she uses here is …*
- *The effect of this/these aspect(s) …*
- *A third aspect used to explore the [insert specific description of the response to the surroundings] is [insert aspect] evidenced in this example [quote], which means …*
- *The reason for this is …*
- *This highlights … because …*
- *The writer wants us to consider … because …*

> **Poet vs Writer vs Author – which label to use?**
> Writer and author cover ALL text types; only use 'poet' when discussing the person who has written a poem.

COMPARING TEXTS

To develop our understanding of any text, a really useful tool is to compare it with another text. By looking for the similarities and differences, one can appreciate more thoroughly the skill used to communicate a message.

In this section, we want to show you some simple steps to apply when you are asked to compare texts.

Step 1: Analyse the question
Be very clear what specific aspect you are being asked to consider and stick to looking at this only.
Look for key words in both texts which relate to the question.

Step 2: Identify similarities and differences in the content
Start with what is similar and discuss then look for the differences.
Consider the reason why these differences exist.

Step 3: Identify similarities and differences in the construction of the texts
Look at the start and the end of the text.
Consider the development of the ideas.
Consider aspects such as setting, style, character, point of view.
Look at the use of language features/techniques.

Step 4: Identify similarities and differences in purpose
The tone and word choice are a clue to the purpose.
Consider if the writer achieves their purpose. Why or why not?

Step 5: Evaluate the effectiveness of each
This is an opportunity for you to bring in your own opinion so long as you support what you say with specific discussion linked directly to the texts.

The most effective way to think about the structure of your comparison discussion is to imagine you are swinging two jump ropes, one clockwise and the other anti-clockwise: swing your right arm out and up and then your left arm out and up as you swing your right arm back down and in. The way you discuss the two texts is like this: in other words, talk about one text, then talk about the second text then back to the first text then on to the second text again. Repeat over.

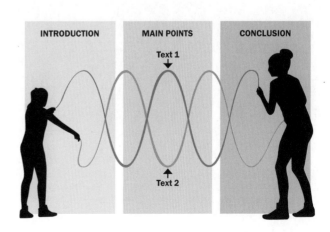

1 Using the step-by-step guide on page 25 fill in the Venn diagrams below for steps 2, 3, and 4.

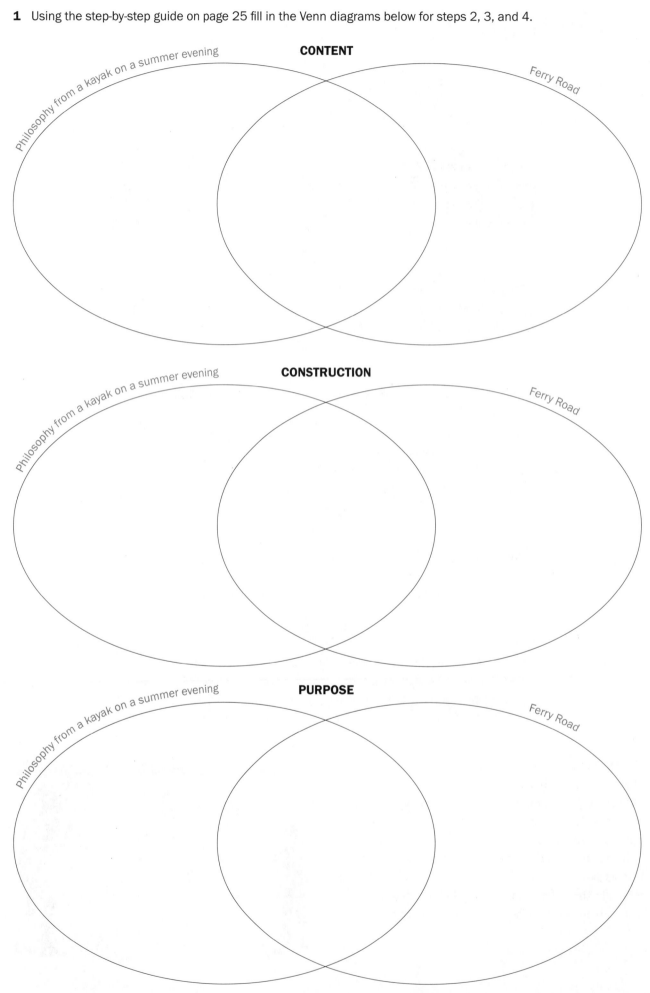

CONTENT

Philosophy from a kayak on a summer evening

Ferry Road

CONSTRUCTION

Philosophy from a kayak on a summer evening

Ferry Road

PURPOSE

Philosophy from a kayak on a summer evening

Ferry Road

Putting it together

When you compare texts, it's important to talk about both texts all the way through. In each paragraph, make sure you mention both, even if a point is mostly about one of them.

When comparing texts, you are making a point about two different texts, backing up ideas with evidence and explaining the idea. Then using a linking statement, you can connect the two ideas together.

Some key phrases can help you to compare texts.

Similarities	Differences
Similarly, ...	In contrast, ...
Equally, ...	However, ...
In the same way, ...	On the other hand, ...
Just as ..., so does ...	Alternatively, ...
Both ... and ...	In a different way, ...

QUESTION THREE

Compare how the writers portray how people respond to the landscape, referring to at least ONE specific aspect used in each text.

Aspects may include personification, syntax, listing, use of te reo Māori.

If you require more space to complete your answer, please move on to your own paper and attach it to this page.

SET 2

Now that you have worked through the first two texts, we will be starting to remove some of the pre-reading activities. This doesn't mean that they are no longer important, but, rather, we are hoping that you are starting to work through them naturally yourself as you read the text. Remember to pay attention to the language used, the title, and your first impressions.

PROSE: *The Wrong One* by Chiao Lin

Reading the text

Read the text through once, taking your time, and out loud if possible. Underline or circle any words you are unsure of or words which 'catch your eye'. Perhaps put a question mark (?) next to anything you do not understand.

The Wrong One

Lily returned home on Friday afternoon with her cousin Leah. Her room was up the stairs but Leah's three younger brothers were in the way. They got the afternoon off school and were already absorbed in their game, jostling each other and tumbling on the floor.

If it had been Leah, or her own sister Anna, Lily would've stepped right over. Easy as pie. But she couldn't now; they were boys. They could walk over her as they liked, but her turn had never been and would never come. There were lots of things that didn't make sense.

No matter how many times she opened the book hidden in the corner of the library, she couldn't understand DNA and chromosomes, and weren't X and Y letters of the alphabet? The book told fibs because there was no way a tiny dot could make all the difference in the world.

Instead, she ventured into the kitchen where her mother was cleaning up.

'Good, Lily, you're home. Don't forget the vendor's coming in ten minutes – Grandpa will expect you children to be there.'

Lily hadn't forgotten. Treats didn't come by often. If only. 'Mama? Do you think I can get a pork bun today?' Nothing was audible over the washing of the dishes. 'Not every time,' Lily added hastily. 'Just once.' She fiddled with the cuff of her right sleeve. It was fraying.

Her mother glanced her way. 'Stop it. Your sisters ...' she broke off. 'Anna needs the shirt after you grow out of it.'

The boys had moved away from the stairs so Lily headed for her room. No sooner had she swung her satchel off her shoulder than the door opened.

Anna came in, her face flushed. 'Sissy, I took all of Grandpa's money.'

'You what?' Lily stared at her.

Anna. Little Anna who could barely see over the top of the table. 'He made me look after the shop when he went out. Said there was no one else 'cos you and Leah weren't back yet. Look!' She held out her hands. 'We've got so much money now!' Her fists were full of large fifty-yuan coins, medium ten-yuan coins and heaps of tiny one-yuan coins.

'No, Anna, that's not right.' Lily's heart thumped. Painfully. 'When did you take it?'

'Just now.' Anna looked up. The tears were starting to form. 'But it's not fair, Sissy.'

Lily grabbed her sister's hand and ran down the stairs, past their mother in the kitchen and around the boys playing on the floor.

The shop sat opposite their house. All was silent when they entered. The knot in Lily's chest lessened. Maybe there was a chance they wouldn't get into trouble. It was just like any other day, nothing amiss except for the empty jar on the counter. She quickly helped her sister return the money. If anything happened, Lily would be the one held responsible.

She was the eldest after all; she wasn't three, or four, but five years older than Anna. She should know better. The doorbell chimed suddenly. But only their father appeared, back from the harbour where he worked.

'You're early, Dad,' announced Lily as Anna let go of the last coin with a chink. She beamed despite herself. Mama wouldn't make them wait for dinner tonight.

He gave a start. 'What are you two doing in the dark?' He shook his head. 'Never mind.' He took a tattered cloth bag out of his pockets and emptied its contents into the jar.

They crossed the street as the familiar shout of 'Freshly steamed buns for sale! Pork buns for fifteen yuans and vegetable buns for ten!' came to their ears. The vendor approached, pushing his trolley of goods.

Grandpa came out, followed by the three boys and Leah. Lily and Anna joined their cousins, unnoticed.

Grandpa handed money over to the vendor and the children lined up to collect their buns as a family tradition. Lily focused her gaze on each pair of hands when her younger cousins sauntered past, one by one.

They were the lucky ones. They always got what they wanted, what she wanted.

A white bun with a red dot.

That was how the vendor told the buns apart, like the way a farmer might mark the ears of his cows.

A second white bun with a red dot. Another white bun with a red dot. Leah stepped up to the trolley and then it was Lily's turn. She held her hands out.

'There you go, Missy.' The weight of the bun made Lily's fingers curl instinctively around it; she was always scared she would drop it.

It was still hot. If she pressed any harder, her fingernails would make indents in the dough. It was that soft. Lily looked up. The vendor was waiting for her to go, so he could serve Anna and leave for his next customer. 'Thank you, Mister,' she said softly. Slowly, Lily relaxed her fingers. Mama didn't believe in the saying 'third time lucky'. Lily wasn't sure yet. Could the luck still work after goodness knows how many times?

There on her palms nestled a white bun. Completely white. It was beautiful, was it not? Smooth and flawless; this one was a real treat. Lily had tried so hard, waited for so long. She could smell the aroma of spices, the sweetness of the dough.

What difference did the little red dot make?

She would love it all the same.

Chiao Lin

Immediate response

1 Use the space below to record your first impressions. You can jot down singular words, phrases and/or ideas.

2 What aspect of the text did you most engage with? What will you remember?

3 What does it make *you* think about?

_____

_____

_____

_____

4 How would a second reading be different? What would you focus on the next time you read the piece?

_____

_____

_____

_____

5 How would different people view this text differently (dependent on gender, age, ethnic background, worldview, etc.)?

_____

_____

_____

_____

Post-reading questions

Read the text again.

1 a Circle the word that you think best describes Lily's family income:

poor   average   affluent

b Write down a quote that reinforces your selection above.

_____

2 Find at least two lines from the first two paragraphs that let us know that boys are treated differently to girls in this family.

_____

_____

3 Why do you think Anna steals the money from the shop? (A clue is that when Lily reacts badly, Anna says 'But it's not fair, Sissy.')

_____

_____

_____

4 In paragraph 22 Lily states 'They always got what they wanted, what she wanted.'

a Who are 'they'? _____

b What is it that Lily wants? _____

c Why do you think Lily doesn't get it? _____

5 Lily ends the story by saying 'What difference did the little red dot make? / She would love it all the same.' Who is she trying to convince here and do you think it works?

_____

_____

Unpacking the text

1 IDENTIFYING THE TONE

a What types of feelings and atmosphere does this piece create for you?

_____

_____

_____

b Reread the text and:
  i Highlight, using differing colours, positive and negative words and phrases.
  ii Organise the positive and negative words and phrases into two lists.

Positive	Negative

  iii Look at the words listed above. Describe the tone of the passage. Do not use the words 'positive' or 'negative'. Be more specific, e.g. 'resentful', 'hopeful', 'nervous', 'funny'.

  The tone is mostly _____ because of words such as _____

  _____

  _____.

c Identify the main subject/topic of the text.

_____

d Write down a quote that describes (or shows) the subject.

_____

e Describe the writer's attitude to the subject. Use examples from the text to support your answer.

The writer is _____ because

she uses words like _____ when describing

_____.

These words make the reader think about _____

_____ because _____

_____

_____.

Identifying and discussing the effects of how the story is communicated

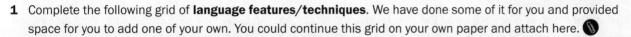

1 Complete the following grid of **language features/techniques**. We have done some of it for you and provided space for you to add one of your own. You could continue this grid on your own paper and attach here.

Technique	Example(s)	Effect	Why it is effective	How does this develop our understanding of the writer's purpose?
Rhetorical question	'What difference did the little red dot make?'			Lily is trying to convince herself that it doesn't matter that she didn't get the pork bun. That the bun she got was lovely. But we all know that actually the answer is that it means everything. No one should be treated differently to another on grounds of appearance.
Alliteration	'No **s**ooner had **s**he **s**wung her **s**atchel off her **s**houlder'	Builds a sense of quick movement.		
Simile	'That was how the vendor told the buns apart, like the way a farmer might mark the ears of his cows.'			An interesting comparison. Perhaps the author is saying that how a prize cow might be identified by its tag, so a pork bun can be identified.

Language focus: Repetition

Because the writer cannot be standing at your shoulder pointing out parts of their piece they want you to notice, they employ techniques which will highlight certain words or phrases. One of these techniques is repetition. Repeating a word (or phrase) tells us that the word is important enough to be repeated and lets us know that we are to pay close attention to the section of text and the language used. It is especially important to notice if there are any changes around other words or punctuation within the repeated section. If words or phrases are repeated in a poem or piece of prose, ask yourself:

Who is speaking?
Why is this word or phrase important to the narrator? (The answer to this 'why' will be related to the overall purpose of the piece.)

There are some special types of repetition and they have really weird names. Here they are below.

> **Epizeuxis:** repeating words in a sequence, e.g. 'Go, go, go!'
>
> **Anaphora:** repeating words at the beginning of a sentence or phrase, e.g. *Don't* play with your food, *don't* spend all your pocket money, *don't* annoy the dog.
>
> **Epistrophe:** repeating words at the end of a sentence of phrase, e.g. I bought you chocolate *because you asked me to*, I bought you flowers *because you asked me to*, I waited at the bus stop *because you asked me to*. I am a good friend.
>
> **Mesodiplosis:** repeating words in the middle of a sentence, e.g. I'll tidy my room *before* I leave, feed the cat *before* I leave, and I'll switch off the lights *before* I lock the door. Promise.

1 Look closely at the excerpt from the text below, identify the type of repetition used and discuss its effect.

> A white bun <u>with a red dot.</u>
> That was how the vendor told the buns apart, like the way a farmer might mark the ears of his cows.
> A second white bun <u>with a red dot.</u> Another white bun <u>with a red dot.</u> Leah stepped up to the trolley and then it was Lily's turn. She held her hands out.

a What type of repetition is this? _____

b What is the intended effect? _____

 ISBN: 9780170454445

Putting it together

QUESTION ONE
Discuss the way in which the writer reflects on how the children are treated, referring to at least TWO specific aspects of written text.

Aspects may include imagery, sentence lengths, alliteration, simile.

You should start your answer using the words of the question. If you are stuck, you can use some of the sentence starters on pages 14 or 23.

_____

_____

_____

_____

_____

_____

_____

_____

_____

_____

_____

_____

_____

_____

_____

_____

_____

_____

_____

_____

_____

_____

_____

_____

_____

_____

If you require more space to complete your answer, please move on to your own paper and attach it to this page.

POEM: *Mother* by Renee Liang

Reading the text

Read the poem, out loud if possible. Read down the columns, not across, i.e. Brain, then Lung, then Heart, etc. Then read it again making any annotations that come instinctively to you: question marks, words/images which stand out, etc.

Mother

Brain

the eldest sister
she raised
her brothers
showed her sister

how to cook
for others first
but now she's far
from those crowded streets

instead she's on
an unfamiliar island

her wedding ring
still shiny
her husband
holding her at night.

Lung

cartoon dogs
on flannel sheets
wag at the rain
challenge grass clippings

inside
she vacuums
broken porcelain
from the new orange carpet

finds a discarded bib
in the corner

listens
for the first cry
from the
small bedroom.

Heart

she measures
the rice
three cups
for five mouths

slices meat
from chicken bones
to stir-fry
with choy sum

lays chopsticks
on white plates

says not to worry
she's last
to sit down
at table.

Liver

he works at the hospital
until 10 pm
wants dinner hot
when he gets home

they have two girls
and one on the way
he asks her to learn
to drive

her words boil
like soup

she swallows
picks up
the swat
to kill flies instead.

Spleen

from the new house
she can see the school
she's learning the names
of the friends' parents

her children
come home
with words
she's never heard

she wonders whether
to ask them to explain

pays for music lessons
buys a cake to take
to the school stall
learns to make party jelly.

Kidney

today
after thirty seven years
the last daughter
leaves the house

three empty beds
faded floral curtains
a wardrobe still full
of teenage dresses

a car arrives
small feet patter

she runs past
the new high chair
opens the door
to the sound of 'Por-por'.*

Renee Liang

Por-por = Cantonese term for maternal grandmother.

Immediate response

1 Use the space below to record your first impressions. You can jot down singular words, phrases and/or ideas.

2 What aspect of the text did you most engage with? What will you remember?

3 What does it make *you* think about?

4 How would different people view this poem differently (dependent on gender, age, ethnic background, worldview, etc.)?

Unpacking the text

1 IDENTIFYING THE TONE

a What types of feelings and atmosphere does this piece create for you?

_____

_____

_____

b Reread the text and:
  i Highlight, using differing colours, positive and negative words and phrases.
  ii Organise the positive and negative words and phrases into two lists.

Positive	Negative

  iii Look at the words listed above. Describe the tone of the poem. Do not use the words 'positive' or 'negative'. Be more specific, e.g. 'resentful', 'hopeful', 'nervous', 'funny'.

  The tone is mostly _____ because of words such as _____

  _____

  _____ .

c Identify the main subject/topic of the poem.

_____

d Write down a quote that describes (or shows) the subject.

_____

_____

e Describe the writer's attitude to the subject. Use examples from the poem to support your answer.

The writer is _____ because

she uses words like _____ when describing

_____ .

These words make the reader think about _____

_____ because _____

_____

_____ .

A closer look at the structure

> Renee Liang says of this poem '[This is] the latest in a series of sonnet sequences I am writing about people close to me, exploring cultural beliefs to do with organ systems.'

Consider the literal as well as figurative connotations of these organs. Choose TWO and write a statement comparing the meaning of the subheading and the subject matter of the words beneath. We have done the first one as an example for you.

1 Name of organ: _Brain_

Literal: _The most complex of organs which is the control centre for our nervous system and is located inside the skull._

Figurative: _Our thoughts, memories, decision making, logic, knowledge._

Discussion: _Perhaps as the eldest in the family she is seen as the wisest one and also the one who controls what her siblings are to do._

2 Name of organ: _____

Literal: _____

Figurative: _____

Discussion: _____

3 Name of organ: _____

Literal: _____

Figurative: _____

Discussion: _____

Identifying and discussing the effects of how the poetry sequence is communicated

1 The following **language features/techniques** can be found in the poem. Find and label on the text (on page 36) an example of each of the techniques in the box below. Refer to the glossary (at the back of the book) if you do not know these words.

> alliteration   personification   adjectives   repetition   sibilance   onomatopoeia

2 Complete the following grid of **language features/techniques**. We have done some of it for you and provided space for you to add one of your own. You could continue this grid on your own paper and attach here.

Technique	Example(s)	Effect	Why it is effective	How does this develop our understanding of the writer's purpose?
Extended metaphor of all the sonnets together	Each sonnet is given a title based on organ systems (brain, heart, liver, etc.)	The sonnets build a bigger poem between them.	The images/words echo and build on each other through the sequence.	Just as there are several levels in our lives/narrative/life course, there is also the development of character through the interaction of the two previous.
	'cartoon dogs / on flannel sheets / wag at the rain / challenge grass clippings'	Creates a sense that the sheets are alive/it is childlike.		
Repetition		Stands out among the other words. Connects the stanzas.	Suggests a sense that it is unfamiliar – like the 'unfamiliar island' in the third stanza.	

Technique	Example(s)	Effect	Why it is effective	How does this develop our understanding of the writer's purpose?
Sibilance	'she swallows / picks up / the swat / to kill flies instead.'		This is a harsh sound and how we might image she is letting out air, hissing, like releasing pressure in a tyre or balloon.	

Language focus: Imagery – Simile

Writers want to show us what it is they are 'seeing' in their imagination and must use words which create pictures in *our* minds. This technique is called the use of imagery. Imagery is used to make a text more vivid – as close as possible to the picture the author has in their head about what they are writing about. There are many devices writers use to do this. In this section we are touching on the **simile**.

The **simile** compares two things using the words 'like', 'as', and sometimes 'than' to compare and contrast something. A famous simile is Robbie Burns' 'O my love is like a red, red rose.' The two things being compared are the poet's love and a red rose. Our job, as the reader, is to make deeper connections between the two objects being compared. For example, Burns could be referring to 'love' as a person as well as an emotion. If we consider both meanings of the word 'love' and consider the word 'rose', we can say that they are lovely to look at, precious, take a while to grow, can hurt you, not everyone can grow love/roses, etc.

1 Identify the simile in the poem *Mother*.

_____

2 List what the two things have in common.

_____

_____

_____

3 Explain why you think these two things have been chosen for the simile. Discuss in light of the overall message.

_____

_____

_____

Putting it together

QUESTION TWO

Discuss the way in which the writer reflects on the role of immigrant women, referring to at least TWO specific aspects of written text.

Aspects may include extended metaphor, personification, repetition, sibilance.

If you require more space to complete your answer, please move on to your own paper and attach it to this page.

COMPARING TEXTS

To prepare for this answer, plan your response on some extra paper, using the steps and Venn diagrams on pages 25 and 26 as a guide.

QUESTION THREE

Compare how the writers portray the way men and women are regarded, referring to at least ONE specific aspect used in each text.

Aspects may include imagery, metaphor, sibilance, repetition.

_____

_____

_____

_____

_____

_____

_____

_____

_____

_____

_____

_____

_____

_____

_____

_____

_____

_____

_____

_____

_____

_____

_____

_____

_____

_____

_____

_____

_____

_____

If you require more space to complete your answer, please move on to your own paper and attach it to this page.

PROSE: from *The Absolute Book* by Elizabeth Knox

from *The Absolute Book*

Taryn was curled up on cushions piled in the bay window. The day was dull, and for the past hour she had bent ever closer to her book while tilting its pages to the light.

Of the many stories Taryn had read about only children – lonely onlys, or plucky girls with odd ways of reasonings; about orphans in attics, or hidden demigods with the weight of the world on their shoulders – this book was the best. The girl in the book was the same age as Taryn, who was ten, and at the beginning the girl was doing the same thing she was, sitting on a window seat, in a fine old house, reading, while outside it rained and rained. Before Taryn got very far in, she pulled the curtains closed, exiling herself from the warm room, the library lamps and the fire her grandfather had laid, one of coal heaped over the white bricks that Taryn's Kiwi grandmother called 'little Lucifers', though the packet read 'Strike-a-Fire'.

Wind joined the rain. Raindrops blew right in under the portico to hit the window, forming glassy freckles on its dust powdered surface. It was the kind of weather that made Taryn think the sun was shining nowhere, though her parents were probably right now sitting on a restaurant terrace above the sea in Antibes drinking pink wine. Her father would be eyeing up anyone 'with a bit of vivacity' as he put it, from behind dark glasses to be sure, but always transparent to Taryn whenever she was around to monitor him. Taryn's father's looking didn't always lead to anything, but he was forever perusing the menu.

Taryn was cold behind the curtain. It was cold in her book too, in the locked room with a girl who had been sent to think on her ingratitude. Taryn understood that the Red Room's cold was worse than that of her grandfather's house though Princess Gate's upper floors were now only waterproof in four bedrooms.

Any moment now a ghost would appear. And a ghost would mean the whole story would be friendlier to wild girls than stuffy adults.

Taryn raised her eyes from the page to savour the moment before the ghost arrived and changed the story. She saw the wind sweeping yellow leaves into the angle between the terrace and wall. She screwed up her eyes. How did one perform 'passionate weeping'? She could ask her father, but then he might demonstrate rather than explain, and that was always embarrassing.

Then the curtain was pulled back and Taryn was discovered – not by John Reid, Jane Eyre's bullying cousin, but by her sister. Beatrice climbed onto the window seat and pinched the curtains closed. She met Taryn's eyes and put a finger to her lips.

Who were they hiding from? Grandma was at her veterinary practice and Grandfather had taken a few of his many dozen notebooks away to the kitchen to review a chapter of his history of this house, leaving the girls in the library.

The library was Princess Gate's most distinguished room. It was carpeted in old silk rugs pinned down by heavy oak furniture. Its shelves had sliding library ladders. There were glass front cabinets full of faded butterflies, giant shells and withered pufferfish. The huge globe labelled in gilt lettering no longer swivelled – hadn't since, years ago, a school friend of their mother had rolled it down the lawn and into the lake. There were deep shelves full of scroll cases. And, of course, there were the books, many of them leather-bound classics, some welcoming to young readers, *Kidnapped* and *Ivanhoe*, *Black Arrow* and *Jane Eyre*. Grandfather could get a little peace if, on their visits, he ceded the girls his library. He didn't mind disobliging himself or the man he liked to call, in a lavish way, his secretary.

Elizabeth Knox

QUESTION ONE

Discuss the way in which the writer explores how the character responds to her surroundings, referring to at least TWO specific aspects of written text.

Aspects may include adjectives, repetition, listing, personification, syntax.

_____

_____

_____

_____

_____

_____

_____

_____

_____

_____

_____

_____

_____

_____

_____

_____

_____

_____

_____

_____

_____

_____

_____

_____

_____

_____

_____

_____

_____

_____

_____

_____

_____

_____

If you require more space to complete your answer, please move on to your own paper and attach it to this page.

POEM: *Fairy Tale* by Fiona Farrell

Fairy Tale

There were two sisters in the story.
Remember? One dark, one fair. And a
bear who came in to lie by the fire.
So they learned early that appearances
5   deceive and that it's wise to be polite
to hags and goblins. Kiss the frogs.
You just can't tell in forests where
light flickers and reality can change
in seconds. And one night the dark
10   sister walked out and met death who
wasn't old as they expected: dim and
toothless, dwindling to decay but a
young man riding who gathered her up
wild into the storm. And the fair one
15   seeks her still in daffodils and all
bright vivid things because she knows
that in this forest shapes shift, fit on
new skins, but nothing vanishes
completely. The right words said with
20   love can spring a sudden transformation.

So she lives. We hope happily.
And we hope ever after.

Fiona Farrell

QUESTION TWO

Discuss the way in which the poet explores the impact fairy tales have on people, referring to at least TWO specific aspects of written text.

Aspects may include rhetorical questions, repetition, cliché, allusion.

_____

_____

_____

_____

_____

_____

_____

If you require more space to complete your answer, please move on to your own paper and attach it to this page.

COMPARING TEXTS

To prepare for this answer, plan your response on some extra paper, using the steps and Venn diagrams on pages 25 and 26 as a guide.

QUESTION THREE

Compare how the writers portray the relationship between sisters, referring to at least ONE specific aspect used in each text.

Aspects may include alliteration, contrast, rhetorical question, personal pronoun, symbolism.

If you require more space to complete your answer, please move on to your own paper and attach it to this page.

Chapter **Two**: PEOPLE

SET 1

PROSE: from *How We Fell* by Glenn Colquhoun

Pre-reading activities

Before beginning any analysis of a text, it is a good idea to complete some pre-reading activities. Pre-reading activities are designed to kick-start your brain, allowing you to reach into it and consider things you know but that you may have forgotten about. Activating your brain before reading a text you've never seen before helps you understand the text in more detail from the first reading.

1 PREDICTING

a Write the definition of each of these short, simple words in the title:

  i   How _____

  ii We _____

  iii Fell _____

b What do you think is the subject matter of the text? This is called predicting.

_____

_____

_____

Reading the text

Below are two extracts from the collection of short prose and poems, *How We Fell* by Glenn Colquhoun. Read them through once, taking your time, and out loud if possible. Underline or circle any words you are unsure of or words which 'catch your eye'. Perhaps put a question mark (?) next to anything you do not understand.

Extract A

How We Fell

1   I didn't mean to fall in love when I did. I met somebody remarkable. For a while the sky was purple. There were twelve moons. When people talked their mouths moved so slowly you could see a man putting words between them as if he was keeping a scoreboard.

2   I didn't mean to fall out of love either. Ten years later I stared at the sky from flat on my back and wondered how I fell there.

3   The earth was soft. The tides were reliable. I wanted to tell her about it but I couldn't.

4   Every season since, I pass each of these doorways at least once and remember living between them.

Extract B

The castle that we built

5   Down Tui Road we carried a brown lounge suite up a flight of stairs, over the balcony, through the window, onto the floor, then sat on it like a summit. We had no flags. But the pub was noisy on Friday night and Club Raro on Saturday. On Sunday we walked over broken glass. We promised each other we would.

6   Near Preston Road I built a place to keep her clothes. They hung like a hedge with occasional flowers. Her skin was apple. The neighbour was mad. We painted the kitchen to keep it clean. Behind a fence the motorway barked like a dog.

7   At Redoubt Road we made love silently, scared of the walls and the people behind them. Tip-toeing along its secret paths we rested our bikes on the grass, climbed the fence, folded our clothes and held our breath. Throwing back our heads and laughing all the harder for the lack of noise we made, we listened to my sisters argue in the bathroom.

8   Along St George Street we hunted dragons, one by one from battlements we found at first unkempt. We filled the walls with noise, scrubbing the roof, sanding the doors, polishing the floors until they throbbed, sleeping while they creaked at night, every sound familiar, cramming them with details of ourselves and, forever after that leaving them haunted.

Glenn Colquhoun

Immediate response

1 Write down your first impressions of each extract.

Extract A: _____

_____

Extract B: _____

_____

2 Consider your prediction from the pre-reading activities (page 49). What is similar? Different? What are your thoughts about how 'close' your prediction(s) were?

_____

_____

_____

_____

Unpacking the text

1 THE TITLE UNLOCKED

The title of a text will have a figurative and a literal meaning. The literal meaning will tell you about the **subject** of the text and the figurative meaning will tell you about the **theme** and/or **purpose** of the text.

You have already considered the words in the title. Now we want you to think about the possible meanings in light of what you now know.

a Look closely again at each word and consider what the titles mean. We have completed the first one for you:

Literal meaning
Falling to the ground. An accident that happened (in the past). The way something happened, two or more people fell.

'How We Fell'

Figurative meaning
Making a mistake. Falling in love. Getting tricked into something.

Literal meaning

'The castle that we built'

Figurative meaning

b Complete the following:

How We Fell means [literal meaning] _____

_____ and also means [figurative meaning]

_____.

This is an appropriate title for the first extract because _____

_____.

The title of the second extract, The castle that we built refers to [literal meaning] _____

_____ and also means [figurative meaning] _____

_____.

This is an appropriate title because _____

_____.

2 IDENTIFYING THE TONE

Tone, in written composition, is an attitude of a writer towards a subject or an audience. Tone is generally conveyed through the choice of words, or the viewpoint of a writer on a particular subject. Every written piece covers a central theme or subject matter. The manner in which a writer approaches this theme and subject is the tone. The tone can be formal, informal, serious, comic, sarcastic, sad, or cheerful, or it may be any other existing attitude.

Source: https://literarydevices.net/tone/

a Reread the text and:

  i Highlight, using differing colours, positive and negative words and phrases.

  ii Organise the positive and negative words and phrases into two lists.

Positive	Negative

  iii Look at the words listed above. Describe the tone of the passage. Do not use the words 'positive' or 'negative'. Be more specific, e.g. 'resentful', 'hopeful', 'nervous', 'funny'.

  The tone is mostly _____ because of words such as _____

  _____

  _____

b Identify the main subject/topic of the text.

  _____

c Write down a quote that describes (or shows) the subject.

  _____

  _____

d Describe the writer's attitude to the subject. Use examples from the text to support your answer.

  The writer is _____ because

  he uses words like _____ when describing

  _____

  These words make the reader think about _____

  _____ because _____

  _____

  _____

  _____

  _____

3 FIND THE PATTERN

A writer selects the order, pace, and manner in which information is communicated to the reader. They do this because they want us to 'read' their work in a particular way. Identifying the structure of a text adds to our understanding of the purpose.

Each paragraph contains a central idea or point that relates to the overall purpose of the passage. Glenn Colquhoun is 'building' his argument/explanation about how his relationship began and ended and what happened in between. Looking at the individual pieces is part of what we call *unpacking the text and is a key skill in being able to critically analyse.*

a Choose five paragraphs and summarise the idea in one sentence – turn it into an assertion if you are able to. We would also like you to jot down your own opinion as to what you think of the assertion. Write the number of the paragraph in the space provided. We have done the first one for you.

Paragraph _1_ : _He fell in love unintentionally and it was so unexpected that it altered the way he saw the natural world._

My thoughts on this idea: _Falling in love changes the way you see things and messes with your mind._

_____

Paragraph _____: _____

_____

My thoughts on this idea: _____

_____

_____

Paragraph _____: _____

_____

My thoughts on this idea: _____

_____

_____

Paragraph _____: _____

_____

My thoughts on this idea: _____

_____

_____

Paragraph _____: _____

_____

My thoughts on this idea: _____

_____

_____

b What is it that the writer wants us to learn/know/understand about this relationship? Why do you think he believes it important that we know this? You can use our sentence starters or write your own on a separate piece of paper and attach to this page.

The writer wants us to understand that _____

because _____

_____.

It's important we understand this/his truth so that/because _____

_____

_____.

Identifying and discussing the effects of how the passages are communicated

We have deliberately waited until near the end of your analysis to get you to identify techniques. This is because it is crucial that you **understand the ideas** in the passages in detail prior to understanding **how** they are communicated.

Identifying the **subject** and **tone** of the passage like you did in the earlier activities helps you understand the writer's purpose. This purpose is then communicated through a variety of **language features** or **language techniques**. These terms are used interchangeably in this book.

1 Complete the following grid of **language features/techniques**. We have done some of it for you and provided space for you to add one of your own. You could continue this grid on your own paper and attach here. 🖉

Technique	Example(s)	Effect	Why it is effective	How does this develop our understanding of the writer's purpose?
Imagery	'the motorway barked like a dog'	It is a sharp, harsh, annoying noise.		A warning, like a dog letting people know there is danger, this image foreshadows the 'bad end' to their relationship.
	'The tides were reliable'	Illustrates that the event would happen as expected.		Connected to the idea of the cycle of the natural world that things come and go, like this relationship, like these tides.
Sound techniques: assonance, alliteration, sibilance	'**m**ouths **m**oved **s**o **s**lowly'	The 'oh' and 'oou' sounds mimic ...		
	'**s**ilently, **s**cared of the wall**s**'	The 'sss' sound mimics someone whispering.		
Parallel construction	'I didn't mean to fall in love ... I didn't mean to fall out of love'			

2 Answer these focus questions.

a Explain the significance of starting the text 'How We Fell' with the personal pronoun 'I' and ending paragraph 4 with 'them'?

_____

_____

b What do the sentences 'For a while the sky was purple. There were twelve moons.' tell us about the writer's state of mind?

_____

_____

_____

c Discuss the meaning and effect of the following sentences from paragraph 6:
'Near Preston Road I built a place to keep her clothes. They hung like a hedge with occasional flowers.'

_____

_____

_____

Language focus: Adverbs/adverbial phrases

An adverb tells the reader when, how, and where an action takes place.

A phrase is a group of words. So, an adverbial phrase is a group of words designed to provide specific detail about an action.

Some adverbs are: slowly; yesterday; somewhere.

Some examples of adverbial phrase: stretching **stiffly and with discomfort**; she finished her work **as quickly as possible**'.

1 List TWO adverbs/adverbial phrases from the extracts and, for each one, describe the effect it has on the structure of the piece and explain how it contributes to the overall message of the passage. We have done the first one for you.

a **'For a while':** This is telling us that the activity went on for a time but has now stopped. It did not last. The word 'while' suggests it could be a long time. The effect of this is to set up that the start of the relationship 'distorted' the writer's view of the world but it didn't last.

b _____

_____

_____

_____

c _____

_____

_____

Putting it together

QUESTION ONE

Discuss the way in which the writer explores the nature of his relationship, referring to at least TWO specific aspects of written text.

Aspects may include imagery, sound techniques, parallel construction, proper noun.

Let's first take a moment to understand what it is the question is asking you to do. It is useful to annotate the question to remind yourself to address each aspect in your answer. We have done this for you this time.

> Means specific techniques/aspects used, including structure/tone/word choice.

> This is 'the what' you need to talk about.

Discuss the way **in which the writer** explores the nature of his relationship, **referring to at least TWO specific aspects of written text.**

> This means you must provide specific, accurate, relevant points – with examples and explanation of the aspects as they relate to the nature of his relationship.

You should start your answer using the words of the question.

If you are stuck, you can use some of the sentence starters below:

- *The writer wants to tell us about what happened to end his relationship because …*
- *The writer takes us through the life (and death) cycle of his relationship …*
- *His attitude towards love/his relationship is …*
- *The writer uses [insert name of aspect] when he says [insert quote] to show …*
- *Another technique he uses here is …*
- *The effect of this/these aspect(s) …*
- *A third aspect used to explore the [insert specific description of the relationship] is [insert aspect] evidenced in this example [quote], which means …*
- *The reason for this is …*
- *This highlights … because …*
- *The writer wants us to consider … because …*

     ISBN: 9780170454445

POEM: *Near Death Experience* by John Allison

Pre-reading activities

The same as with a prose piece, before beginning any analysis of poetry, it is a good idea to complete some pre-reading activities. Pre-reading activities are designed to kick-start your brain, allowing you to reach into it and consider things you know that you may have forgotten about.

1 PREDICTING

a What is the phenomenon of a 'near-death experience'? If you do not know, research this.

_____

_____

b What do you think is the subject matter of the text?

_____

_____

Reading the text

Read the poem, out loud if possible. And then read it again making any annotations that come instinctively to you: question marks, words/images which stand out, etc.

Near Death Experience

At times like these she opens up
his drawer and takes out
his favourite shirt. Unfolding it,
she holds it out in front of her
5   as though trying it
against him standing there.
And for a long time she is seeing
him again, his eyes,
his quick smile, his chest
10   against which she laid her head,
his arms enfolding her.
The whole smell and taste of him.
She feels the once familiar
changes, how her skin is gloved
15   by his touch, her body
an enclosure he turns inside out.
She feels these changes.
She is a tree, standing in a forest
fire. The foliage dissolves,
20   her limbs are sheathed in flame.
She feels the breath go out of her.

The fire passes, and she is
ash, incandescent, sinking, ash.
The sun is setting. She is
25   holding the shirt still.
Carefully she folds it, puts it back
again, into his drawer.
Again. It slides shut so easily.

John Allison

Immediate response

1 Write down your first impressions of the poem.

_____

_____

_____

2 Consider your prediction (on page 58). What is similar? Different? What are your thoughts about how 'close' your prediction(s) were?

_____

_____

_____

_____

_____

Unpacking the text

1 THE TITLE UNLOCKED

The title of a text will have a figurative and a literal meaning. The literal meaning will tell you about the **subject** of the text and the figurative meaning will tell you about the **theme** and/or **purpose** of the text.

You have already considered the words in the title. Now we want you to think about the possible meanings in light of what you now know.

a Look closely again at each word and consider the title.

Literal meaning	Figurative meaning

'Near Death
Experience'

b Complete the following:

Near Death Experience means [literal meaning] _____

_____ and also means [figurative meaning]

_____.

This is an appropriate title for the poem because _____

_____.

2 IDENTIFYING THE TONE

Tone, in written composition, is an attitude of a writer towards a subject or an audience. Tone is generally conveyed through the choice of words, or the viewpoint of a writer on a particular subject. Every written piece covers a central theme or subject matter. The manner in which a writer approaches this theme and subject is the tone. The tone can be formal, informal, serious, comic, sarcastic, sad, or cheerful, or it may be any other existing attitude.

Source: https://literarydevices.net/tone/

a What types of feelings and atmosphere does this piece create for you?

_____

_____

_____

b Reread the text and:
  i Highlight, using differing colours, positive and negative words and phrases.
  ii Organise the positive and negative words and phrases into two lists.

Positive	Negative

  iii Look at the words listed above. Describe the tone of the poem. Do not use the words 'positive' or 'negative'. Be more specific, e.g. 'resentful', 'hopeful', 'nervous', 'funny'.

  The tone is mostly _____ because of words such as _____

  _____

  _____.

c Identify the main subject/topic of the poem.

_____

d Write down a quote that describes (or shows) the subject.

_____

_____

e Describe the writer's attitude to the subject. Use examples from the poem to support your answer.

The writer is _____ because

he uses words like _____ when describing

_____ .

These words make the reader think about _____

_____ because _____

_____

_____ .

Identifying the 'point of change'

All fiction (poetry and narrative prose) has a 'point of change' in it. The point of change shows us the writer's **attitude** towards the subject, which helps us understand the writer's purpose. Identifying and understanding the point of change is a strategy used to analyse the poem.

1 Identify the line where the point of change occurs. _____

2 Describe the atmosphere before this change. _____

_____

_____

3 Identify two words that contribute to this atmosphere.

a _____ **b** _____

4 Describe what the atmosphere is after the change. _____

_____

_____

Summarise

1 In no more than two sentences, write what this poem is about.

_____

_____

_____

2 Complete the following sentence.

The poet wanted to teach us about _____

_____ because [you should include a description of

what the poet wants us to learn/know/understand about our world/about life and why we need to learn this]

_____

_____

_____ .

Point of view

'Who' tells the story affects how the story is told: the selection of details, the order information is conveyed, the tone. Often the piece is from the point of view (POV) of the writer but not always. In this poem, the POV is a 'she'.

1 What are the advantages and disadvantages of an author writing with a difference 'voice'?

_____

_____

_____

_____

Identifying and discussing the effects of how the poem is communicated

Identifying the **tone** and **point of change** of the poem like you did in the earlier activities helps you understand the poet's purpose. This purpose is then communicated through a variety of **language features** or **language techniques**. These terms are used interchangeably in this book.

1 The following **language features/techniques** can be found in the poem. Find and label on the text (on pages 58–59) an example of each of the techniques in the box below. Refer to the glossary (at the back of the book) if you do not know these words.

| metaphor | listing | adjectives | possessive pronoun |
| use of present tense | minor sentence | repetition | |

2 Complete the following grid of **language features/techniques**. We have done some of it for you and provided space for you to add one of your own. You could continue this grid on your own paper and attach here. ✎

Technique	Example(s)	Effect	Why it is effective	How does this develop our understanding of the writer's purpose?
Metaphor	'her skin is gloved / by his touch,' 'she is a tree ...'	A glove is soft and covers a hand in protection. Represents growth and strength and endurance.		
Listing	'she is / ash, incandescent, sinking, ash.'			

Technique	Example(s)	Effect	Why it is effective	How does this develop our understanding of the writer's purpose?
Possessive pronoun	his her			
Incomplete/ minor sentence	'The whole smell and taste of him.'			

Language focus: 'Present participle' and 'the gerund'

Both these grammatical techniques have the suffix 'ing' at the end of the word but only the **present participle** functions as a verb (doing word) in the sentence. It is used to suggest continuous action.

Some present participles from the poem are: **Unfolding** it; **enfolding** her; she is **seeing** him.

In comparison, a **gerund** is treated as a noun (naming word) in the sentence.

Some examples of gerund: She is a tree, **standing in a forest fire**; against him **standing** there.

1 List TWO present participles from the poem and describe the overall effect these have on the **tone and rhythm** of the poem.

List	Effect

Putting it together

QUESTION TWO

Discuss the way in which the writer explores the nature of loss, referring to at least TWO specific aspects of written text.

Aspects may include metaphor, listing, possessive pronoun, incomplete/minor sentence.

Let's first take a moment to understand what it is the question is asking you to do. It is useful to annotate the question to remind yourself to address each aspect in your answer. We have done this for you this time.

> Means specific techniques/aspects used, including structure/tone/word choice.

> This is 'the what' you need to talk about.

Discuss **the** way in which **the writer** explores the nature of loss, **referring to at least TWO specific aspects of written text.**

> This means you must provide specific, accurate, relevant points – with examples and explanation of the aspects as they relate to the nature of loss.

You should start your answer using the words of the question. If you are stuck, you can use some of the sentence starters below:

- *The writer wants to tell us about what it can be like for the person experiencing the loss of a partner because …*
- *The writer takes us through the cycle of these feelings …*
- *The poet's attitude towards love/relationships is …*
- *The writer uses [insert name of aspect] when he says [insert quote] to show …*
- *Another technique he uses here is …*
- *The effect of this/these aspect(s) …*
- *A third aspect used to explore the [insert specific description of the relationship] is [insert aspect] evidenced in this example [quote], which means …*
- *The reason for this is …*
- *This highlights … because …*
- *The writer wants us to consider … because …*

COMPARING TEXTS

To develop our understanding of any text, a really useful tool is to compare it with another text. By looking for the similarities and differences, one can appreciate more thoroughly the skill used to communicate a message.

In this section, we want to show you some simple steps to apply when you are asked to compare texts.

Step 1: Analyse the question
Be very clear what specific aspect you are being asked to consider and stick to looking at this only.
Look for key words in both texts which relate to the question.

Step 2: Identify similarities and differences in the content
Start with what is similar and discuss then look for the differences.
Consider the reason why these differences exist.

Step 3: Identify similarities and differences in the construction of the texts
Look at the start and the end of the text.
Consider the development of the ideas.
Consider aspects such as setting, style, character, point of view.
Look at the use of language features/techniques.

Step 4: Identify similarities and differences in purpose
The tone and word choice are a clue to the purpose.
Consider if the writer achieves their purpose. Why or why not?

Step 5: Evaluate the effectiveness of each
This is an opportunity for you to bring in your own opinion so long as you support what you say with specific discussion linked directly to the texts.

The most effective way to think about the structure of your comparison discussion is to imagine you are swinging two jump ropes, one clockwise and the other anti-clockwise: swing your right arm out and up and then your left arm out and up as you swing your right down and in. The way you discuss the two texts is like this: in other words, talk about one text, then talk about the second text then back to the first text then on to the second text again. Repeat over.

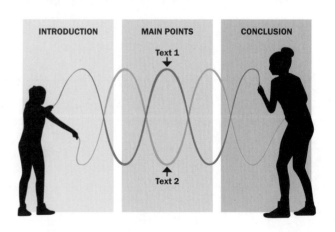

1 Using the step-by-step guide on page 66 fill in the Venn diagrams below for steps 2, 3, and 4.

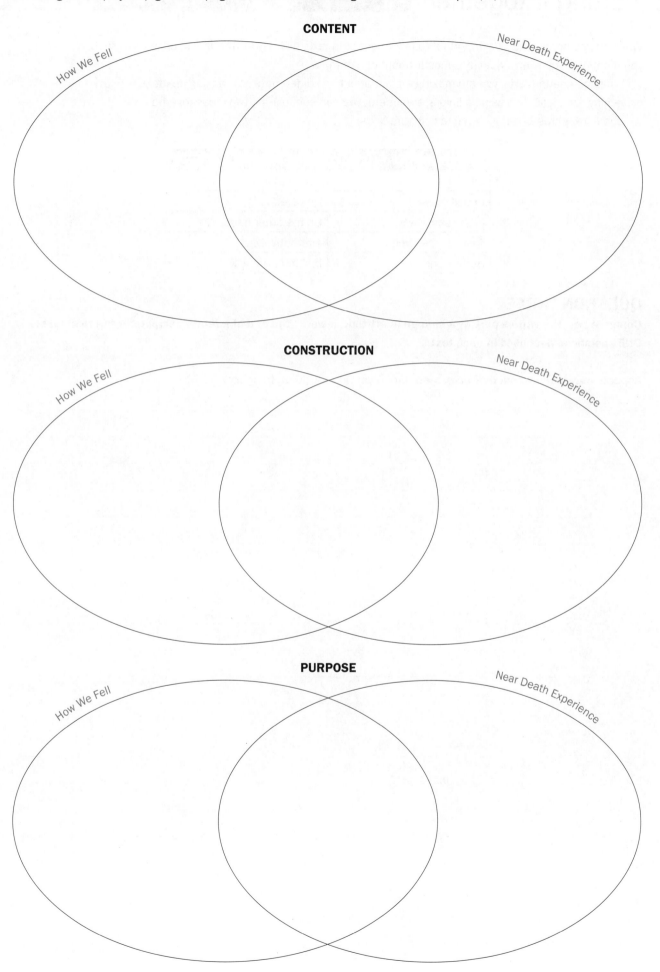

CONTENT

How We Fell

Near Death Experience

CONSTRUCTION

How We Fell

Near Death Experience

PURPOSE

How We Fell

Near Death Experience

ISBN: 9780170454445

Putting it together

When you compare texts, it's important to talk about both texts all the way through. In each paragraph, make sure you mention both, even if a point is mostly about one of them.

When comparing texts, you are making a point about two different texts, backing up ideas with evidence and explaining the idea. Then using a linking statement, you can connect the two ideas together.

Some key phrases can help you to compare texts.

Similarities	Differences
Similarly, …	In contrast, …
Equally, …	However, …
In the same way, …	On the other hand, …
Just as …, so does …	Alternatively, …
Both … and …	In a different way, …

QUESTION THREE

Compare how the writers portray a change in attitude towards the end of a relationship, referring to at least ONE specific aspect used in each text.

Aspects may include sound effects, metaphor, syntax, repetition, imagery.

If you require more space to complete your answer, please move on to your own paper and attach it to this page.

SET 2

Now that you have worked through the first two texts, we will be starting to remove some of the pre-reading activities. This doesn't mean that they are no longer important, but, rather, we are hoping that you are starting to work through them naturally yourself as you read the text. Remember to pay attention to the language used, the title, and your first impressions.

PROSE: from *The Writing Teacher* by T.K. Roxborogh

Reading the text

Read the text through once, taking your time, and out loud if possible. Underline or circle any words you are unsure of or words which 'catch your eye'. Perhaps put a question mark (?) next to anything you do not understand.

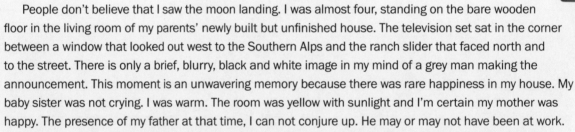

from *The Writing Teacher*

People don't believe that I saw the moon landing. I was almost four, standing on the bare wooden floor in the living room of my parents' newly built but unfinished house. The television set sat in the corner between a window that looked out west to the Southern Alps and the ranch slider that faced north and to the street. There is only a brief, blurry, black and white image in my mind of a grey man making the announcement. This moment is an unwavering memory because there was rare happiness in my house. My baby sister was not crying. I was warm. The room was yellow with sunlight and I'm certain my mother was happy. The presence of my father at that time, I can not conjure up. He may or may not have been at work.

Later, there would be photos and news stories and film footage played and replayed through the media and displayed in text books but I've batted those away from my child self's moment in time. Brain specialists and child psychologists would argue it's impossible for one to remember this far back; that somehow the 'memory' has been planted. To them I say, 'Bite me! I know what I know.'

I lived in that house in Burwood from my birth until our mother sent us away to my grandmother's. The memories of that time are strange and staccato. Like a photo that had been exposed twice, is the picture of this home when I was small: both sunlight and cold-blue – running to the window of my parents' bedroom to see the mountain covered with snow, and playing outside on the underdeveloped lawn with the boy up the street who could kill a Daddy Long Legs with his bare hand.

In another memory, I walk down the hallway. And, as I approach the pool of light let in by the back door, I cover the side of my face so I won't see the broken glass and the blood. I knew it was there. I'd heard the yelling, heard the axe, heard the door shatter and Mum crying.

I cannot recall the whole thing so I have filled in the gaps with what I suppose was the real story of domestic abuse and unhappiness. Still, what remains is shadowing my face with a hand as I run quickly past the door.

Memories too of my father in the kitchen: *How many chocolate bars do you want?* he'd asked, kneeling in front of me. I'd held up three fingers making my parents laugh. I liked this sound that swelled around me without the sour smell of booze.

There were cousins all around us, from the Kelly side: once a trip with them to a frozen lake to skate. A big boy fell; his foot slipped through the ice, freezing his toes. *Frost bite*, my father said. *Bad luck.* I watched my big boy cousin cry while the St John's Ambulance nurse wrapped his toes. I'd eyed that dull, solid surface certain the shadow of the frost monster moved under our booted feet. Dad picked me up and carried me to the snow-covered banks. I must have been crying because he wiped the coarse sleeve of his bush jacket across my face. The next thing I remember is coming down the hill in the sledge with him in front. The echo of giggles as ticklish as bubbles sits hushed but pleased inside my mind.

Then he was in hospital. A factory accident. *Daddy has a burnt bum. Daddy has a burnt bum.* Maybe it was me who sang this or my older sister. Neither of us know now who it was but we do recall the speckled cheeks of his bottom shimmering under the hospital lights. Mum told him off. Dad winked and we both felt *very* pleased to be included in his naughtiness.

Then he leaves. Or, we do.

No more night trips to blinking yellow lights on the road sides or to places with tall silver houses. Sober, he was the sweetest fella; soaked with beer, he was stroppy, maudlin, and violent. Like the time he rolled his car and, when people came to his aid, he pulled a shot gun on them. Maybe it was at this point of my story when my father went to prison. Or, it may have been one too many 'drunk in charge of a vehicle' convictions. Or just simply drunk again. My big sister, Donna, waited for him every day, standing alone outside against the letter box. If I imagine this picture, it is only because my mother often told people of how long Donna waited there. She tells me it was a long time. And that she cried.

To me, it was like the noise got switched off so that it was suddenly quiet. Not just in sound but in feeling too. For a short time at least.

T.K. Roxborogh

Immediate response

1 Use the space below to record your first impressions. You can jot down singular words, phrases and/or ideas.

2 What aspect of the text did you most engage with? What will you remember?

3 What does it make *you* think about?

4 How would a second reading be different? What would you focus on the next time you read the piece?

5 How would different people view this text differently (dependent on gender, age, ethnic background, worldview, etc.)?

_____

_____

_____

Post-reading questions

Read the text again.

1 Give an opinion. Tell us what you think or feel about a certain part of this story and why. Be specific.

_____

_____

_____

_____

_____

2 Why do you think the author/narrator starts with the moon landing? What is the point that is being made here?

_____

_____

_____

_____

3 Choose two words that describe how the narrator feels about her father and choose two quotes to back up your choice.

Word 1: _____   Word 2: _____

Quote 1: _____   Quote 2: _____

_____   _____

_____   _____

4 Circle the word that you think best describes the topic of this text.

memories   relationships   abuse   childhood

Explain in no less than three sentences why you chose this word: _____

_____

_____

_____

_____

_____

_____

Unpacking the text

1 IDENTIFYING THE TONE

a What types of feelings and atmosphere does this piece create for you?

_____

_____

_____

b Reread the text and:
- **i** Highlight, using differing colours, positive and negative words and phrases.
- **ii** Organise the positive and negative words and phrases into two lists.

Positive	Negative

iii Look at the words listed above. Describe the tone of the passage. Do not use the words 'positive' or 'negative'. Be more specific, e.g. 'resentful', 'hopeful', 'nervous', 'funny'.

The tone is mostly _____ because of words such as _____

_____.

c Identify the main subject/topic of the text.

_____

d Write down a quote that describes (or shows) the subject.

_____

_____

e Describe the writer's attitude to the subject. Use examples from the text to support your answer.

The writer is _____ because

she uses words like _____ when describing

_____.

These words make the reader think about _____

_____ because _____

_____

_____

_____.

Identifying and discussing the effects of how the passage is communicated

1 Complete the following grid of **language features/techniques**. We have done some of it for you and provided space for you to add one of your own. You could continue this grid on your own paper and attach here.

Technique	Example(s)	Effect	Why it is effective	How does this develop our understanding of the writer's purpose?
Imagery	'bare wooden floor … living room … newly built but unfinished house.' '… coarse sleeve of his bush jacket across my face.'			She argues that psychologists believe young children have faulty memories but the specifics used in this imagery give authority to her assertion that she does in fact remember the moon landing as these events happened around the same time.
Alliteration/ sibilance	'**st**range and **st**accato.' '**s**ound that **s**welled around me without the **s**our **s**mell of booze.'	Draws attention to the words; the hissing sound mimics a snake's/negative or painful gasp or noise.		
Repetition	'*Daddy has a burnt bum. Daddy has a burnt bum.*'			
Contrast (of memories)	'heard the door shatter' and next '*How many chocolate bars do you want?*'		Shows that there were happy moments when he asked her the question about getting the treat but that there were terrible moments as well.	

PHOTOCOPYING OF THIS PAGE IS RESTRICTED UNDER LAW.   ISBN: 9780170454445

Language focus: Sentence types

Imagine that the writer is a road traffic controller but instead of flags or gloved hands and a whistle to direct how and when cars may move along a stretch of road, the writer must use a variety of sentence types to control how fast or slow you read their work. The main types of sentences we will look at closely now.

The simple sentence (aka **independent clause**) is a name for a sentence that can make complete sense from the beginning to the full stop. It must contain a subject (a thing or person who does the action) and a verb (action). It often will have an object (but does not have to). Another name for a simple sentence is 'main clause' or 'interdependent clause'.

e.g. People don't believe that I saw the moon landing.

A compound sentence is the name for a sentence that contains two or more simple sentences (independent clauses) joined by coordinating conjunctions (FANBOYS – for, and, nor, but, or, yet, so – and also the semicolon ;).

e.g. The room was yellow with sunlight and I'm certain my mother was happy.

A minor sentence is a group of words that do not make sense on their own. It needs a simple sentence to make it complete. There are two main types of minor sentences:

i   **the phrase**: a group of words without a verb, e.g. 'A factory accident'.

ii **the subordinate clause**. Sometimes, a sentence does have a verb but it still does not make sense on its own, e.g. 'Like a photo that had been exposed twice'. Subordinate means something or someone lower than something or someone else, like a private in the army is subordinate to a sergeant. These subordinate clauses also need a simple sentence to complete the meaning.

The complex sentence is one simple sentence joined to one or more subordinate clauses.

e.g. 'I was almost four, standing on the bare wooden floor in the living room of my parent's newly built but unfinished house.'

1   Label the following sentences as either simple, compound, complex, or subordinate clause.

a   For a short time at least. _____

b   Mum told him off. _____

c   Dad winked and we both felt *very* pleased to be included in his naughtiness. _____

d   I liked this sound that swelled around me without the sour smell of booze. _____

When analysing texts, look for the effect the sentence types have on the mood/tone/atmosphere of the piece. The length and rhythm of the sentence, the syntax and word choice all should work together to enhance the overall imagery of the narrative.

2   Choose one of the sentences above (or any other from the text) and explain how the type of sentence matches the purpose or content of the sentence.

For example: *For a short time at least.* This sentence is short and does not have a verb (therefore is a phrase). This fits with the meaning because the sentence is describing something that does not go on for long.

_____

_____

_____

Putting it together

QUESTION ONE

Discuss the way in which the writer explores her feelings about her early memories, referring to at least TWO specific aspects of written text.

Aspects may include imagery, alliteration, repetition, contrast.

You should start your answer using the words of the question. If you are stuck, you can use some of the sentence starters on page 56 or 64.

If you require more space to complete your answer, please move on to your own paper and attach it to this page.

POEM: *My Father Today* by Sam Hunt

Reading the text

Read the poem, out loud if possible. Then read it again making any annotations that come instinctively to you: question marks, words/images which stand out, etc.

My Father Today

They buried him today
up Schnapper Rock Road,
my father in cold clay.

A heavy south wind towed
5   the drape of light away.
Friends, men met on the road,

stood round in that dumb way
men stand when lost for words.
There was nothing to say.

10   I heard the bitchy chords
of magpies in an old-man
pine ... My old man, he's worlds

away – call it Heaven –
no man so elegantly
15   dressed. His last afternoon,

staring out to sea,
he nods off in his chair.
He wonders what the

yelling's all about up there.
20   They just about explode!
And now, these magpies here

up Schnapper Rock Road ...
They buried him in clay.
He was a heavy load,

25   my dead father today.

Sam Hunt

Immediate response

1 Use the space below to record your first impressions. You can jot down singular words, phrases and/or ideas.

2 What aspect of the text did you most engage with? What will you remember?

3 What does it make *you* think about?

4 How would different people view this poem differently (dependent on gender, age, ethnic background, worldview, etc.)?

Unpacking the text

1 IDENTIFYING THE TONE

a What types of feelings and atmosphere does this piece create for you?

b Reread the text and:

   i Highlight, using differing colours, positive and negative words and phrases.

   ii Organise the positive and negative words and phrases into two lists.

Positive	Negative

   iii Look at the words listed above. Describe the tone of the poem. Do not use the words 'positive' or 'negative'. Be more specific, e.g. 'resentful', 'hopeful', 'nervous', 'funny'.

The tone is mostly _____ because of words such as _____

_____

_____.

c Identify the main subject/topic of the poem.

_____

d Write down a quote that describes (or shows) the subject.

_____

_____

e Describe the writer's attitude to the subject. Use examples from the poem to support your answer.

The writer is _____ because

he uses words like _____ when describing

_____.

These words make the reader think about _____

_____ because _____

_____

_____

_____

Identifying and discussing the effects of how the poem is communicated

1 The following **language features/techniques** can be found in the poem. Find and label on the text (on page 77) an example of each of the techniques in the box below. Refer to the glossary (at the back of the book) if you do not know these words.

> alliteration   imagery   personification   adjectives
> proper nouns   parallel structure/book ending

2 Complete the following grid of **language features/techniques**. We have done some of it for you and provided space for you to add one of your own. You could continue this grid on your own paper and attach here. 📎

Technique	Example(s)	Effect	Why it is effective	How does this develop our understanding of the writer's purpose?
Alliteration	'cold clay'	Really emphasises the imagery and the negative nature of where the poet's father is being buried.	Helps us imagine the sadness of the moment. The coffin isn't going into dirt but rather a chalky-coloured, cold and heavy clay. Clay, where things struggle to grow.	
Imagery		Helps us visualise in our mind.	We feel like we are really there with Hunt, alongside him as he buries his father. We know that it is windy, dark and that his father is being buried in cold clay.	
Parallel structure/book ending	'They buried him today / up Schnapper Rock Road, / my father in cold clay.' and 'up Schnapper Rock Road… / They buried him in clay. / He was a heavy load, / my dead father today.'		Adds a nice sense of symmetry to the poem, and a sense of closure.	

Technique	Example(s)	Effect	Why it is effective	How does this develop our understanding of the writer's purpose?
Repetition	'my father' 'My old man' 'old-man / pine' 'dead father'		All words that are quite disconnected – 'father' rather than 'daddy'. 'My old man' can be seen as a term of endearment but in this poem, it seems more like a holding back, creating a sense of space between the two. Old man pine is a particular type of pine – drawing comparisons to the old man pine which is stuck in one place and now Hunt's old man who is buried in this one place too but is 'worlds away'.	

Language focus: Allusion

This language technique assumes the reader has some prior knowledge of the ideas, objects, people and/or places being referred to. It is a useful technique to communicate a lot of information in a reduced space.

Allusion: where a word or phrase refers to a well-known person or event therefore providing extra background information to enhance the message or feelings of the piece.

e.g. 'He becomes a Romeo when they walk in the room.'

The descriptor 'Romeo' is an allusion to the Shakespearean play *Romeo and Juliet*. At first sight of Juliet, Romeo falls quickly and passionately in love and behaves in a manner that ultimately leads to tragedy.

1 Investigate the following allusions from the poem:

a my father in cold clay

_____

b of magpies in an old-man / pine

_____

c He was a heavy load

_____

Putting it together

QUESTION TWO

Discuss the way in which the poet reflects on his father's funeral, referring to at least TWO specific aspects of written text.

Aspects may include alliteration, imagery, parallel structure/book ending.

You should start your answer using the words of the question. If you are stuck, you can use some of the sentence starters on page 56 or 64.

_____

_____

_____

_____

_____

_____

_____

_____

_____

_____

_____

_____

_____

_____

_____

_____

_____

_____

_____

_____

_____

_____

_____

_____

_____

_____

_____

If you require more space to complete your answer, please move on to your own paper and attach it to this page.

COMPARING TEXTS

To prepare for this answer, plan your response on some extra paper, using the steps and Venn diagrams on pages 66 and 67 as a guide.

QUESTION THREE
Compare how the writers portray their fathers, referring to at least ONE specific aspect used in each text.

Aspects may include repetition, allusion, imagery, contrast.

_____
_____
_____
_____
_____
_____
_____
_____
_____
_____
_____
_____
_____
_____
_____
_____
_____
_____
_____
_____
_____
_____
_____
_____
_____
_____
_____
_____

If you require more space to complete your answer, please move on to your own paper and attach it to this page. ●

Now that you have completed the activities on the first four texts, you are ready to attempt a set as if you were under exam conditions. Using all of the skills you have been practising throughout this section, give the following questions your best shot. For each one put your timer on for 20 minutes. Read the piece and use your strategies to answer the question. Good luck!

PROSE: from *Double Take* by Emma Neale

from *Double Take*

Peas in a pod. Cherries on a stem. Jeffrey and Candy. A pair, a set, a perfect match, people seemed to so quickly think, looking from sister to brother and recalling stories from the *Woman's Weekly* or *Time* about twins who communicate in private code: cryptophasia, idioglossia, or ESP. They saw Candy and Jeff and thought of siblings studied by linguists, psychologists, even anthropologists; as if twins were a tribe of two with a secret understanding, existing in a self-contained, mysterious world. 'Yep, my two pearls,' their dad would say to those who asked. Years later Candy would sometimes feel she was still up against the ogling curiosity: a scientist on the Net saying she envied the parents of twins, 'who have instant access to this living laboratory!' or the front page story in a regional newspaper that announced: "Flaw in Gene Responsible: Twins a Biological 'Mistake'"; or magazine headlines: "Nepalese Baby Girl Twins Separated by Surgeons", "Film Star's Miracle Twins". If twins were in it, it was twice the news, apparently.

'Aren't they sweet!' creaked elderly couples in the mall, making Candy feel they wanted to fondle and pick her and Jeff up like novelty salt and pepper shakers displayed in a sale. But how different are salt and pepper if you touch them to your tongue, she thought, looking at Jeffrey's green eyes that reflected her own, the small mole on his left cheek exactly where hers was on the right, the tiny flattening of the bone at the top of the bridge of the nose, as if someone had pressed gently with a thumb into the soft clay of them both before they had fully grown. Identikit, photofit, their mother's womb a copier, trying to perform a duplicate and coming up with boy and girl. Even better than identical twins, relatives said: the perfect family all in one go! A pair, a set, a match. Was it only Candy who came to imagine red flint to strike alight? Or a contest, a series of games, the prize going to the opponent who won the greatest number?

'Oh, they are so obviously twins!' murmured the kindergarten supervisor, the primary school principal, the swimming instructor, the clothes store assistant. 'Fraternal twins,' their mother corrected. 'They're really no more alike than ordinary siblings.' Only nobody listened. The family resemblance was so close – so many of the mirror traits like those of identicals (Candy right-handed, Jeff left; a whorl of Jeff's hair that grew in one direction, Candy's in the other) – that even the GP became excited about the Third-Type-of-Twins hypothesis, waving his hands as he described a theory that the egg can split before conception. Candy saw how Rose's mouth twitched. 'A theory is just that,' she said. 'A theory.'

Yet the resemblance persisted, well after puberty. Even Candy was startled by what happened at a bus stop once, near a downtown construction site, where she and Jeff waited to be collected by Rose. Age sixteen Jeffrey was still boyishly slim, Candy still girlishly flat chested. The dark curls on both their heads reached mid-neck, Jeffrey's tucked behind his ears to show his new silver studs. Candy wore a silver chain with a small guitar pendant. Both twins wore denim jackets and black trousers – Candy's jacket blue, Jeffrey's black. A builder whose yellow hard hat tilted back to show his broad forehead leaned out through some iron girders. 'Gidday, girls,' he grinned. 'Sweet as.'

Jeffrey answered back, voice consciously lowered. 'Gidday mate.'

The builder jerked, his chin tucked in as he stared at them. 'Gender benders. Fucken – poofters!'

(...) 'Right from the start they've been different,' Rose insisted when asked wasn't it difficult raising twins. Twice the work, surely, and wasn't it hard not to see them as a unit? Especially when, if they both wore trousers, and with that curly hair, those South Island river-stone green eyes, the similarity was uncanny. ('Is it a boy or a girl?' asked one four-year-old at kindergarten, looking from Jeffrey to Candy and back again.)

Rose certainly brought some of it on herself. She would insist on dressing them in the same colours. 'Boys' clothes are more practical,' she said, let alone that so often two for the price of one was hard to resist. And it did make the laundry loads so much easier if the children wore the same colours.

Emma Neale

QUESTION ONE

Discuss the way in which the writer explores society's response to the twins, referring to at least TWO specific aspects of written text.

Aspects may include listing, contrast, metaphor, rhythm.

_____

_____

_____

_____

_____

_____

_____

_____

_____

_____

_____

_____

_____

_____

_____

_____

_____

_____

_____

_____

_____

_____

POEM: *For Andrew* by Fleur Adcock

For Andrew

'Will I die?' you ask. And so I enter on
the dutiful exposition of that which you
would rather not know, and I rather not tell you.
To soften my 'Yes' I offer compensations –
5   age and fulfilment ('It's so far away;
you will have children and grandchildren by then')
and indifference ('By then you will not care').
No need: you cannot believe me, convinced
that if you always eat plenty of vegetables,
10   And are careful crossing the street, you will live for ever.
And so we close the subject, with much unsaid –
this, for instance: Though you and I may die
tomorrow or next year, and nothing remain
of our stock, of the unique, preciously-hoarded
15   inimitable genes we carry in us,
it is possible that for many generations
there will exist, sprung from whatever seeds,
children straight-limbed, with clear inquiring voices,
bright-eyed as you. Or so I like to think:
20   sharing in this your childish optimism.

Fleur Adcock

QUESTION TWO

Discuss the way in which the writer explores the mother's feelings about being honest in response to her son's question, referring to at least TWO specific aspects of written text.

Aspects may include question, personal pronoun, parentheses, minor sentences.

_____

_____

_____

_____

_____

_____

_____

_____

_____

_____

_____

_____

COMPARING TEXTS

To prepare for this answer, plan your response on some extra paper, using the steps and Venn diagrams on pages 66 and 67 as a guide.

QUESTION THREE

Compare how the writers portray how mothers respond to their children, referring to at least ONE specific aspect used in each text.

Aspects may include listing, metaphor, contrast, personal pronoun.

_____

_____

_____

_____

_____

_____

_____

_____

_____

_____

_____

_____

_____

_____

_____

_____

_____

_____

_____

_____

_____

_____

_____

_____

_____

_____

_____

_____

_____

_____

_____

_____

_____

If you require more space to complete your answer, please move on to your own paper and attach it to this page.

ChapterThree:
PROBLEMS AND POTENTIAL

SET 1

PROSE: *Whakamā* by Kirsty Dunn

Pre-reading activities

Before beginning any analysis of a text, it is a good idea to complete some pre-reading activities. Pre-reading activities are designed to kick-start your brain, allowing you to reach into it and consider things you know but that you may have forgotten about. Activating your brain before reading a text you've never seen before helps you understand the text in more detail from the first reading.

1 Use your device to find the definition of the word 'whakamā'.

_____

2 What things make you feel whakamā?

_____

_____

Reading the text

Read the text through once, taking your time, and out loud if possible. Underline or circle any words you are unsure of or words which 'catch your eye'. Perhaps put a question mark (?) next to anything you do not understand.

Whakamā

I am perpetually embarrassed.

At Riverhead Primary School Mr Tawhiti comes on Tuesdays to take some of the kids for Māori lessons. We sing waiata and learn kupu and push each other out of the way to get the nicest looking poi to swing around ourselves; the plastic-bag coated balls hit our hands and hips and shoulder blades sounding like a flurry of footsteps. We use rolled-up magazines to play tī rākau, and we think we are cool because we get to do stuff the other kids don't.

At the end of the year, Mr Tawhiti gives me a red plastic Santa boot filled with mini chocolate Santa boots for being his 'best student'.

'Shame,' I hear.

10   'She is such a try hard.'

'Shame' means: shame on her. She should be embarrassed.

I am.

We are having dinner at my Pākehā boyfriend's parents' house. His dad nonchalantly lacerates a

   PHOTOCOPYING OF THIS PAGE IS RESTRICTED UNDER LAW.   ISBN: 9780170454445

Māori place name beyond all recognition. 'That's not how you say it,' my boyfriend says. He breaks the syllables down, slowly (too slowly) accentuating the vowel sounds, trying hard to eliminate room for error. His father is defiant: 'That's how I've always said it.' My boyfriend stares, challenging: 'Well, you've always said it wrong.'

I am embarrassed and want to be anywhere but here, both grateful for the solidarity and exhausted. This is not the first conversation like this, and it will not be the last. (...)

20 Shame is speaking and not being understood. It is not being able to understand when it seems like everyone else can. Shame feels like fluorescent lights and nowhere to hide and a thousand eyes staring and it surges within me as I try to learn the language of my tūpuna. Shame at the thought of needing to do this, shame at the thought of not following through. My vocabulary is limited – but I do know the word whakamā.

Poet Tayi Tibble explains that whakamā, like many kupu, doesn't really have an exact English translation, but that it is akin to 'feelings of inferiority, self-doubt and self-abasement' and is connected with feeling dislocated: of not having 'a sure-footing in te ao Māori'. Dr Kiri Dell draws similar comparisons, noting too that whakamā feels like 'a weakening of oneself' and is related to feelings of inadequacy and disconnection and the many fears and emotions which accompany that.

30 No wonder then, that whakamā is part and parcel of the reo-learning journey for some of us. For to take steps to reclaim the language of our ancestors, is to acknowledge the reasons why reclamation is required in the first place: it is to confront our colonisation, our disconnection and our intergenerational whakamā head on, and sometimes in a public forum.

I start learning te reo Māori. Again. Classes start with karakia (an incantation or prayer) and we share kai and slowly get to know each other and feel a little more comfortable, knowing that at least we are here and trying. I watch as some of my Pākehā classmates kōrero with confidence while some of us remain hesitant. We don't talk about why that is.

I see my kaiako in the supermarket. 'Oh hey, how are you?' I say. 'Kia ora, e hoa. E pai ana au,' he replies – hello, my friend, I am well – and I feel my puku tighten. I have failed to do the only thing 40 required of me in this moment. I have not shown my gratitude for his teaching. I have not put into practice all that I have been at pains to learn.

English is automatic. It is a given. It is ingrained.

And I am so ashamed.

To take steps to reclaim the language of our ancestors is to confront our colonisation, our disconnection and our intergenerational whakamā head on.

Our language, Anahera Gildea reminds us, wasn't simply 'lost', although you will often see this euphemism attached to te reo Māori, implying that we simply misplaced it – how embarrassing for us. 'It was stolen. Not the same. Not equivalent. Not shame.' I think about my grandfather's generation who were physically punished at school for speaking te reo Māori. I think about inherited silences where kōrero should have been. I think about both of these things as I put post-it notes in every corner 50 of our whare, the yellow flags urging me to say their names out loud – moenga, matapihi, paenga, whakaahua. I think about how my feeling whakamā is benefitting some people. I wonder what would happen if I stopped. (...)

'Connection,' writes Kiri Dell, 'is the antidote to whakamā.' But of course it's not just in our shared familiarity with whakamā that this connection is possible. The answer is in the reo itself: our language is relational.

Te reo Māori reveals to us the beauty of whakapapa: the many layers of relationships and connections we carry within us, and the knowledges and worldviews that are embedded within them. It's in the way we introduce ourselves – first by naming the mountain, the river, the waka of our tūpuna, 60 the kinship groups we belong to. It's in our specific words for 'we' and 'yous' and 'them but not us', and the way we talk about our relations – our sisters, brothers, whanaunga. 'Our language', writes Nadine Hura, 'constantly reinforces the understanding that our story is just a small part of a much bigger story'.

In other words, it is about time I got out of my own way.

Kirsty Dunn

Immediate response

1 Write down your first impressions of the article. Discuss the reasons for these impressions.

_____

_____

_____

_____

_____

_____

Unpacking the text

1 THE TITLE UNLOCKED

The title of a text will have a figurative and a literal meaning. The literal meaning will tell you about the **subject** of the text and the figurative meaning will tell you about the **theme** and/or **purpose** of the text. You have already considered the word in the title. Now we want you to think about the possible meanings in light of what you now know.

a Look closely again at the title and consider the different meanings.

Literal meaning

'Whakamā'

Figurative meaning

b Complete the following:

The word 'whakamā' means [literal meaning] _____

_____ and also means [figurative meaning]

_____ .

This is an appropriate title for the piece because _____

_____ .

2 IDENTIFYING THE TONE

Tone, in written composition, is an attitude of a writer towards a subject or an audience. Tone is generally conveyed through the choice of words, or the viewpoint of a writer on a particular subject. Every written piece covers a central theme or subject matter. The manner in which a writer approaches this theme and subject is the tone. The tone can be formal, informal, serious, comic, sarcastic, sad, or cheerful, or it may be any other existing attitude.

Source: https://literarydevices.net/tone/

a   What types of feelings and atmosphere does this piece create for you?

_____

_____

_____

b   Reread the text and:

  i   Highlight, using differing colours, positive and negative words and phrases.

  ii   Organise the positive and negative words and phrases into two lists.

Positive	Negative

  iii   Look at the words listed above. Describe the tone of the passage. Do not use the words 'positive' or 'negative'. Be more specific, e.g. 'resentful', 'hopeful', 'nervous', 'funny'.

The tone is mostly _____ because of words such as _____

_____.

c   Identify the main subject/topic of the text.

_____

d   Write down a quote that describes (or shows) the subject.

_____

_____

e   Describe the writer's attitude to the subject. Use examples from the text to support your answer.

The writer is _____ because

she uses words like _____ when describing

_____.

These words make the reader think about _____

_____ because _____

_____

_____

_____.

3   FIND THE PATTERN

A writer selects the order, pace, and manner in which information is communicated to the reader. They do this because they want us to 'read' their work in a particular way. Identifying the structure of a text adds to our understanding of the purpose.

Each paragraph contains a central idea or point that relates to the overall purpose of the passage. Kirsty Dunn is 'building' her argument/explanation about how colonisation has taken the language from Māori and, as a result, normal, essential connection to place and people has meant a deep-seated feeling of isolation and shame. Looking at the individual pieces is part of what we call _unpacking the text and is a key skill in being able to critically analyse._

a   Look at each section (the line numbers are down the side) and summarise the idea in one sentence – turn it into an assertion if you are able to. We would also like you to jot down your own opinion as to what you think of the assertion. We have done the first one for you.

Lines 1–10: _It doesn't matter if I've done something really great, I still feel ashamed._

My thoughts on this idea: _Often our response to the reactions of others dictates how we feel about ourselves and our achievements._

Lines 11–20: _____

_____

My thoughts on this idea: _____

_____

_____

Lines 21–30: _____

_____

My thoughts on this idea: _____

_____

_____

Lines 31–40: _____

_____

My thoughts on this idea: _____

_____

_____

Lines 41–50: _____

_____

My thoughts on this idea: _____

_____

_____

Lines 51–60: _____

_____

My thoughts on this idea: _____

_____

_____

Lines 61–63: _____

_____

My thoughts on this idea: _____

_____

_____

b What is it that the writer wants us to learn/know/understand about shame? Why do you think she believes it important that we know this? You can use our sentence starters or write your own on a separate piece of paper and attach to this page. 🔗

The writer wants us to understand that _____

because _____

_____.

It's important we understand this/her truth so that/because _____

_____

_____.

Identifying and discussing the effects of how the passage is communicated

We have deliberately waited until near the end of your analysis to get you to identify techniques. This is because it is crucial that you **understand the ideas** in the passage in detail prior to understanding **how** they are communicated.

Identifying the **subject** and **tone** of the passage like you did in the earlier activities helps you understand the writer's purpose. This purpose is then communicated through a variety of **language features** or **language techniques**. These terms are used interchangeably in this book.

1 Complete the following grid of **language features/techniques**. We have done some of it for you and provided space for you to add one of your own. You could continue this grid on your own paper and attach here. 🔗

Technique	Example(s)	Effect	Why it is effective	How does this develop our understanding of the writer's purpose?
Anecdote	'At Riverhead Primary School …'	It is interesting and provides a real-life example to illustrate what she is talking about.	We all like to hear stories of personal experience: this validates her narrative – we all remember our times in primary school.	We get to 'walk in her shoes' because the detail in the anecdote makes us recall times when we have behaved this way and therefore makes the idea of 'shame' universal.
Colloquialism	'try hard' 'Shame'		Everyday language that we hear emphasises that it is a common occurrence.	

Technique	Example(s)	Effect	Why it is effective	How does this develop our understanding of the writer's purpose?
Repetition	'shame' 'our story … bigger story'	Draws attention to the word.		Both the learning of a language and the feelings (positive and negative) which go with it (and the stories that language is soaked in) need constant effort – effort that needs to be repeated. The repetition of the words emphasise both the necessary effort needed to master the language and the unfortunate consequences of feeling shame and embarrassment.
Metaphor	'lacerates a Māori place name beyond all recognition'		The word 'lacerates' conjures up the idea of slicing, cutting, destroying. It has violent connotations. The image is showing how terribly the father has pronounced the name.	

2 Discuss the effect of the underlined phrase. Why do you think it is an appropriate choice of imagery given the tone and subject matter of the article?

> Kirsty Dunn introduces her article with this statement: *Shame is an ever-present part of my life, especially as a Māori language learner trying to regain the words of my ancestors. But in reconnecting with Māori literature, I am learning that shame is not something to be conquered, but to be navigated.*

_____

_____

_____

_____

_____

_____

_____

_____

Language focus: Symbolism

This is where an object represents more than itself, e.g. a cross is a symbol for Christianity, religion, death; a dove is a symbol for peace; a rainbow is the symbol for LGBTQI+.

For each of the examples below, explain what they symbolise.

1 a thousand eyes _____

_____

_____

_____

2 river _____

_____

_____

_____

3 the waka _____

_____

_____

_____

Putting it together

QUESTION ONE

Discuss the way in which the writer explores the reasons people experience shame, referring to at least TWO specific aspects of written text.

Aspects may include anecdote, colloquialism, repetition, metaphor.

Let's first take a moment to understand what it is the question is asking you to do. It is useful to annotate the question to remind yourself to address each aspect in your answer. We have done this for you this time.

> Means specific techniques/aspects used, including structure/tone/word choice.

> This is 'the what' you need to talk about.

Discuss the way **in which the writer** explores the reasons people experience shame, **referring to at least TWO specific aspects of written text.**

> This means you must provide specific, accurate, relevant points – with examples and explanation of the aspects as they relate to her experience of shame.

You should start your answer using the words of the question.

If you are stuck, you can use some of the sentence starters below to help you:

- *The writer wants to tell us about what causes her to feel shame because …*
- *The writer provides specific examples such as [include the examples] because they show us that …*
- *The writer uses [insert name of aspect] when she says [insert quote] to show …*
- *Another technique she uses here is …*
- *The effect of this/these aspect(s) …*
- *The reason for this is …*
- *This highlights … because …*
- *The writer wants us to consider … because …*

POEM: *Feelings and Memories of a Kuia*
by Apirana Taylor

Pre-reading activities

The same as with a prose piece, before beginning any analysis of poetry, it is a good idea to complete some pre-reading activities. Pre-reading activities are designed to kick-start your brain, allowing you to reach into it and consider things you know that you may have forgotten about.

1 PREDICTING

a Use the box below to break down what each word from the title could mean.

Feelings	Memories	Kuia

b From your musings (*thoughts, ponderings, reflections*), what do you think is the subject matter of the text?

_____

_____

_____

Another good pre-reading activity to engage your brain is to make some predictions. Here are two complete stanzas from the poem.

> **Quoting explained**
> **/** indicates a line break in the poetry.

'The bush / got chopped down / the river damned / and the lake polluted'

'Then came the war / I think / a lot of Māori men / who would have been / great leaders / of our people/ got killed overseas / and for what'

c Looking at your musings from question **1b** after breaking down the title, how do these change now you have read two stanzas from the poem?

_____

_____

_____

_____

_____

2 VOCABULARY WORK

Although written in English, this poem is dotted with te reo Māori words. It is important that you know these defintions so you can understand the poem's intent.

For the six words in the grid below, create a sentence that uses it with its correct intention. We have done one for you to start you off.

koro	mokopuna	kuia	kai	ake ake	Pākehā
elderly man; grandfather; grandpa; male elder	grandchildren	elderly woman; grandmother; female elder	to eat; to consume; to devour; food	*Dodonaea viscosa* – a small tree with long, sometimes reddish leaves	English, foreign, European, exotic – introduced from or originating in a foreign country

Definitions sourced from www.maoridictionary.co.nz

a I asked my **koro** to show me how to pump up my bike tyre because Mum and Dad were at work.

b

c

d

e

f

Reading the text

Read the poem, out loud if possible. And then read it again making any annotations that come instinctively to you: question marks, words/images which stand out, etc.

Feelings and Memories of a Kuia

These Māori today
are not Māori any more
I don't know what they are

I remember the old people
5   they were polite
they liked to talk
they walked at a leisurely pace
but always got things done

Today my mokopuna always rush
10   yet never seem to do a thing
they hardly say a word to me
and they don't look happy

When I was a girl
we had big gardens
15   all us children worked in them
and the kuia and koro
used to make jokes
they cooked us a big kai in the morning
we were very happy

20   Sometimes
we went to the lake
we'd get some fern
and tie it into bundles
with ake ake
25   and toss the fern
into the water

When we pulled up the bundles
we'd shake them
and lots of fish
30   would fall out

In the bush
there were plenty
of fat juicy pigeon
the river

35   was full of eels
dinner swam past
all we had to do
was catch it

The bush
40   got chopped down
the river dammed
and the lake polluted

It seems to me
the closer
45   the Pākehā got to us
the more difficult
he made it for us to live

Then came the war
I think
50   a lot of Māori men
who would have been
great leaders
of our people
got killed overseas
55   and for what

So we could live in quarter-acre sections
when once we had
more land
than my eye could see

60   So we could eat
hamburgers
when once we got
fresh kai

So in the end
65   we could be lost
and unhappy
and not know why

Apirana Taylor

Immediate response

1 Use the space below to record your first impressions. You can jot down singular words, phrases and/or ideas.

2 What aspect of the text did you most engage with? What will you remember?

3 What does it make *you* think about?

4 How would different people view this poem differently (dependent on gender, age, ethnic background, worldview, etc.)?

Unpacking the text

1 IDENTIFYING THE TONE

Tone, in written composition, is an attitude of a writer towards a subject or an audience. Tone is generally conveyed through the choice of words, or the viewpoint of a writer on a particular subject. Every written piece covers a central theme or subject matter. The manner in which a writer approaches this theme and subject is the tone. The tone can be formal, informal, serious, comic, sarcastic, sad, or cheerful, or it may be any other existing attitude.

Source: https://literarydevices.net/tone/

a What types of feelings and atmosphere does this piece create for you?

b Reread the text and:

   i Highlight, using differing colours, positive and negative words and phrases.

   ii Organise the positive and negative words and phrases into two lists.

Positive	Negative

   iii Look at the words listed above. Describe the tone of the poem. Do not use the words 'positive' or 'negative'. Be more specific, e.g. 'resentful', 'hopeful', 'nervous', 'funny'.

   The tone is mostly _____ because of words such as _____
_____ .

c Identify the main subject/topic of the poem.

_____

d Write down a quote that describes (or shows) the subject.

_____

_____

e Describe the writer's attitude to the subject. Use examples from the poem to support your answer.

The writer is _____ because

he uses words/phrases like _____ when describing

_____ .

These words make the reader think about _____

_____ because _____

_____

_____ .

Identifying the 'point of change'

All fiction (poetry and narrative prose) has a 'point of change' in it. The point of change shows us the writer's **attitude** towards the subject, which helps us understand the writer's purpose. Identifying and understanding the point of change is a strategy used to analyse the poem.

1 In this poem, there are two points of change, although one is more significant than the other. Identify the lines where the points of change occur.

First: _____ Second: _____

2 Describe the atmosphere before each of these changes.

First: _____

Second: _____

3 Identify two phrases that contribute to this atmosphere before the second change.

a _____   **b** _____

4 Describe what the atmosphere is after the second change.

_____

_____

_____

Summarise

1 In no more than two sentences, write what this poem is about.

_____

_____

_____

2 Complete the following sentence. You should include a description of what the poet wants us to learn/know/ understand about our world/about life and why we need to learn this.

The poet wanted to teach us about _____

_____ because [you should include a description of

what the writer wants us to learn/know/understand about our world/about life and why we need to learn this]

_____

_____

_____

_____

Identifying and discussing the effects of how the poem is communicated

Identifying the **tone** and **point of change** of the poem like you did in the earlier activities helps you understand the poet's purpose. This purpose is then communicated through a variety of **language features** or **language techniques**. These terms are used interchangeably in this book.

1 The following **language features/techniques** can be found in the poem. Find and label on the text (on page 102) an example of each of the techniques in the box below. Refer to the glossary (at the back of the book) if you do not know these words.

personal pronoun	parallel structure	use of te reo Māori	contrast
imagery	past tense	adjectives	rhetorical question

2 Complete the following grid of **language features/techniques**. We have done some of it for you and provided space for you to add one of your own. You could continue this grid on your own paper and attach here. 📎

Technique	Example(s)	Effect	Why it is effective	How does this develop our understanding of the writer's purpose?
Parallel structure	'they were polite / they liked to talk / they walked at a leisurely pace'		Really hammers home the point of how the Māori people have changed since 'the Pākehā got to us'.	
Contrast	'Today my mokopuna always rush / yet never seem to do a thing' 'So we could eat / hamburgers / when once we got / fresh kai'	Clear sense of what has been lost through the imagery created by the contrast.		
Imagery		Similar to above, clear images in the mind of what life was like before the war and the changes that Pākehā wrought on the landscape.		
Past tense	'we went' 'we'd shake' 'there were'		Again, emphasises how things were and what has been lost. Repetition of the communal 'we' also shows how once everyone worked together, as a community.	

Language focus: Irony

Irony is when the message intended is different (usually opposite) to the literal meaning of words used.

Irony is realising the difference between what *is said* and what *is normal or expected*. For example, it is ironic that the kuia talks about a 'fat juicy pigeon' and that 'the river was full of eels' when today a) most 21st-century New Zealanders would not consider this type of food 'delicious' and b) statistics show that food poverty is highest amongst indigenous peoples. The key thing to ask yourself is 'why has the writer used this irony? What is being highlighted and why?'

Irony is the contrast between expectation and reality.

1 Identify one thing that is 'expected' by someone in the poem.

_____

2 What is the reality for this person?

_____

3 Discuss the effect of the contrast between expectation and reality. What is the poet wanting the reader to understand?

_____

_____

_____

_____

_____

Irony is associated with both tragedy and humour.

4 Identify one idea that is 'funny' in the poem and explain the humour.

_____

_____

_____

_____

_____

_____

_____

The difference between irony and sarcasm

Sarcasm is seen as a 'conversational' device and often executed in a mocking or sneering tone. It can be self-deprecating where the writer makes fun of themselves – or it can be directed at the subject. This can also include understatement:

Sarcasm: Yeah, we're doing a great job of looking after the plant. It's only lost 99% of its leaves.

Understatement: Might be a bit warm living near the equator.

The key difference is that sarcasm characterises someone's 'speech' whereas irony can also include situations or someone's circumstances. Some literary critics say that it is more accurate to use the term irony as a literacy device and sarcasm as a way of describing tone.

Putting it together

QUESTION TWO

Discuss the way in which the writer uses contrast to characterise a grandmother figure, referring to at least TWO specific aspects of written text.

Aspects may include parallel structure, contrast, imagery, past tense.

Let's first take a moment to understand what it is the question is asking you to do. It is useful to annotate the question to remind yourself to address each aspect in your answer. We have done this for you this time.

> Means specific techniques/aspects used, including structure/tone/word choice.

> This is 'the what' you need to talk about.

Discuss the way in which the writer uses contrast to characterise a grandmother figure, referring to at least TWO specific aspects of written text.

> This means you must provide specific, accurate, relevant points – with examples and explanation of the aspects as they relate to his characterisation of the kuia.

You should start your answer using the words of the question.

If you are stuck, you can use some of the sentence starters below to help you:

- *The writer notices [insert examples] because …*
- *The writer takes us through …*
- *The poet's attitude towards …*
- *The writer uses [insert name of aspect] when he says [insert quote] to show …*
- *Another technique he uses here is …*
- *The effect of this/these aspect(s) …*
- *A third aspect used to explore the [insert specific description of the response to the surroundings] is [insert aspect] evidenced in this example [quote], which means …*
- *The reason for this is …*
- *This highlights … because …*
- *The writer wants us to consider … because …*

COMPARING TEXTS

To develop our understanding of any text, a really useful tool is to compare it with another text. By looking for the similarities and differences, one can appreciate more thoroughly the skill used to communicate a message.

In this section, we want to show you some simple steps to apply when you are asked to compare texts.

Step 1: Analyse the question
Be very clear what specific aspect you are being asked to consider and stick to looking at this only.
Look for key words in both texts which relate to the question.

Step 2: Identify similarities and differences in the content
Start with what is similar and discuss then look for the differences.
Consider the reason why these differences exist.

Step 3: Identify similarities and differences in the construction of the texts
Look at the start and the end of the text.
Consider the development of the ideas.
Consider aspects such as setting, style, character, point of view.
Look at the use of language features/techniques.

Step 4: Identify similarities and differences in purpose
The tone and word choice are a clue to the purpose.
Consider if the writer achieves their purpose. Why or why not?

Step 5: Evaluate the effectiveness of each
This is an opportunity for you to bring in your own opinion so long as you support what you say with specific discussion linked directly to the texts.

The most effective way to think about the structure of your comparison discussion is to imagine you are swinging two jump ropes, one clockwise and the other anti-clockwise: swing your right arm out and up and then your left arm out and up as you swing your right down and in. The way you discuss the two texts is like this: in other words, talk about one text, then talk about the second text then back to the first text then on to the second text again. Repeat over.

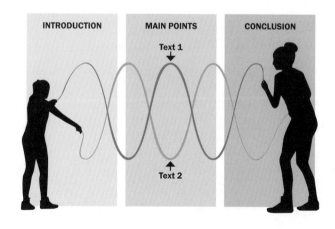

1 Using the step-by-step guide on page 110 fill in the Venn diagrams below for steps 2, 3, and 4.

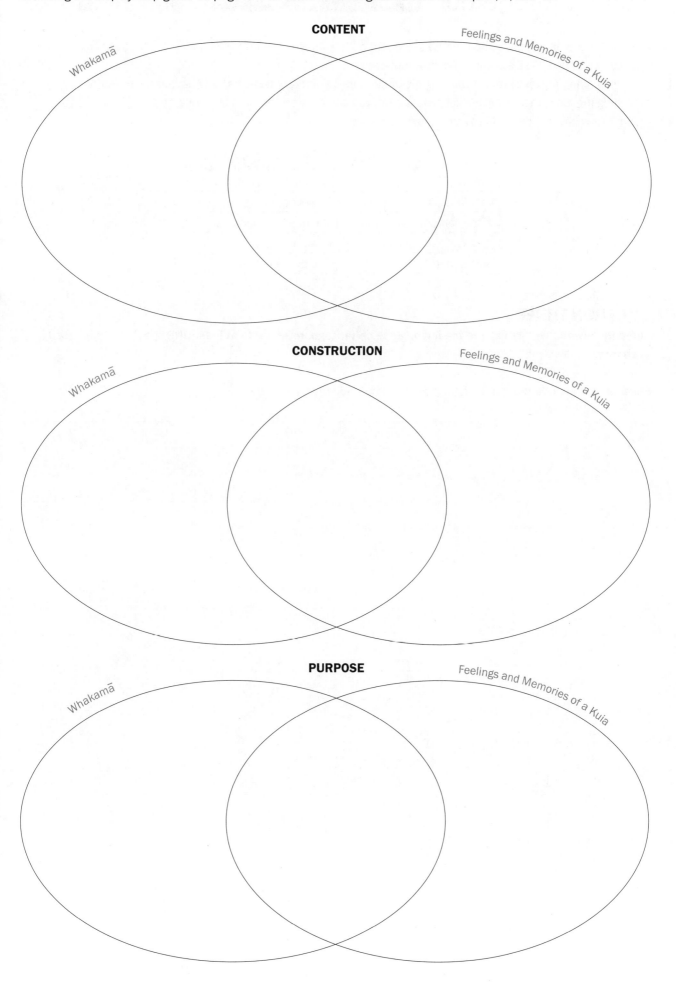

CONTENT

Whakamā

Feelings and Memories of a Kuia

CONSTRUCTION

Whakamā

Feelings and Memories of a Kuia

PURPOSE

Whakamā

Feelings and Memories of a Kuia

Putting it together

When you compare texts, it's important to talk about both texts all the way through. In each paragraph, make sure you mention both, even if a point is mostly about one of them.

When comparing texts, you are making a point about two different texts, backing up ideas with evidence and explaining the idea. Then using a linking statement, you can connect the two ideas together.

Some key phrases can help you to compare texts.

Similarities	Differences
Similarly, ...	In contrast, ...
Equally, ...	However, ...
In the same way, ...	On the other hand, ...
Just as ..., so does ...	Alternatively, ...
Both ... and ...	In a different way, ...

QUESTION THREE

Compare how the writers explore the importance of heritage, referring to at least ONE specific aspect used in each text.

Aspects may include repetition, listing, te reo Māori, adjectives.

_____

_____

_____

_____

_____

_____

_____

_____

_____

_____

_____

_____

_____

_____

_____

_____

_____

_____

_____

_____

_____

_____

If you require more space to complete your answer, please move on to your own paper and attach it to this page.

SET 2

PROSE: *Is it hot enough for you yet?* by David Slack

Reading the text

Read the text through once, taking your time, and out loud if possible. Underline or circle any words you are unsure of or words which 'catch your eye'. Perhaps put a question mark (?) next to anything you do not understand.

Is it hot enough for you yet?

And so that was Christmas.

Across our little collection of islands we came together to be with family and be reminded in between noisy mouthfuls of turkey that the scientists are wrong and some radio host who has opinions for money is right.

It's always a special day for climate change bingo.

'They shouldn't call it climate change. There's always been climate change.'

'We're too small to make a difference. Why doesn't China do something?'

At such moments you may think to yourself: 'gee, reckon the only thing that could change this mind would be if the sky turned to twilight in the middle of the day'.

Blow me down if it didn't happen just a few days later. But never mind the immolation of Australia, they just change the subject to gotcha-you-hypocrite.

'Well Olivia, if you're worried about climate change you'll have to give up all your life's luxuries then. No more plane trips.'

Yes. Let's make the perfect the enemy of the good.

Taking a stand on climate change but not doing every last thing you can does not disqualify your position. Anything that reduces the harm is a step in the right direction. Some things we can do readily, some have to wait for larger change. The way we move around the world would be such an example. Meanwhile you do what you can, and exhort the people who have it in their power to make the large changes.

Why in the face of undeniable truth, do people still grasp at every other possible argument, up to and including complete falsehoods about greens impeding hazard reductions? Is it that the truth is just too inconvenient? That certainly seems the most likely explanation for the abundance of media coverage that serves to protect and preserve the establishment and the status quo.

If you have a sweet number going, well no big surprise if you resist anything that might put it at risk. Is that what the Murdoch media is up to? Does he really believe that's acceptable? Digger please.

Some people fear the unknown and so resist anything that might change the way things are. But doing nothing doesn't mean that things will stay as they are. That option has gone. We have just two choices, they both take us into the unknown, and we have to pick one: give up fossil fuels and move to sustainability, or remain unsustainable and live with the consequences.

Here's the executive summary: the hotter it gets, the worse things are. And it will not be good. It will be awful. Horrible. Deadly. It plays out the IPCC model of a 4 degree Celsius increase in temperatures this century assuming no fossil fuel use change.

Temperature bars reach across the page, moving further and further into the danger zone year after year. In the end those bars come down to something really simple: if nothing changes it will be really, really hot, a whole lot of the time.

By the time a child born today is 20, they say, what we presently think of as extreme would by then be considered a mild summer. By their 50th birthday, three quarters of humanity would be facing at least 20 days a year of deadly heat and humidity. The fundamental point is where those bars are taking us: the hotter it gets, the worse it gets and right now we're seeing how wrong everything can go when it gets too hot.

But if we do act, the future can be better. It really can. The web page underlays the projected bars with the ones we'll see if we can hold the emissions. It's vastly better. There is so much we can do. Electrify everything. Plant more trees. Make public transport free. Produce things on a sustainable basis.

It's knowable, it's doable. If you care about humanity all you have to do is get on board.

And if you just have some angry objection to Greta telling you off, well, this would probably stop her damn whining.

David Slack

Immediate response

1 Use the space below to record your first impressions. You can jot down singular words, phrases and/or ideas.

2 What aspect of the text did you most engage with? What will you remember?

_____

_____

_____

_____

3 What does it make *you* think about?

_____

_____

_____

_____

4 How would a second reading be different? What would you focus on the next time you read the piece?

_____

_____

_____

_____

5 How would different people view this text differently (dependent on gender, age, ethnic background, worldview, etc.)?

_____

_____

_____

_____

Post-reading questions

Read the text again.

1 What picture of the world, and our place in it, is Slack building in this piece? Write your answer in full sentences. Bonus points if you include a quote(s) to back up your points.

_____

_____

_____

_____

_____

_____

_____

_____

_____

2 Why do you think Slack was thinking about these things at Christmas time?

_____

_____

_____

_____

_____

_____

_____

_____

_____

_____

Unpacking the text

1 IDENTIFYING THE TONE

a What types of feelings and atmosphere does this piece create for you?

_____

_____

_____

b Reread the text and:
   i   Highlight, using differing colours, positive and negative words and phrases.
   ii Organise the positive and negative words and phrases into two lists.

Positive	Negative

   iii Look at the words listed above. Describe the tone of the passage. Do not use the words 'positive' or 'negative'. Be more specific, e.g. 'resentful', 'hopeful', 'nervous', 'funny'.

   The tone is mostly _____ because of words such as _____

   _____

   _____.

c Identify the main subject/topic of the text.

_____

d Write down a quote that describes (or shows) the subject.

_____

_____

e Describe the writer's attitude to the subject. Use examples from the text to support your answer.

   The writer is _____ because

   he uses words like _____ when describing

   _____.

   These words make the reader think about _____

   _____ because _____

   _____

   _____.

Identifying and discussing the effects of how the passage is communicated

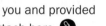

1 Complete the following grid of **language features/techniques**. We have done some of it for you and provided space for you to add one of your own. You could continue this grid on your own paper and attach here. 📎

Technique	Example(s)	Effect	Why it is effective	How does this develop our understanding of the writer's purpose?
Parallel construction	'Some things we can do readily, some have to wait for larger change.'	Contrast/highlights aspects of both parts.		
Quoting others		Acknowledges that everyone is having similar conversations.	Makes us feel like part of a larger whole, that we are all up against 'non-believing' of climate change.	
Imperative	'Plant more trees.' 'Make public transport free.' 'Produce things on a sustainable basis.'			

Language focus: Questions (including rhetorical) and assertions

Both devices are used by writers to engage with their reader/audience by appealing to both the mind and the heart.

> **Questions** in a piece of text cause the reader to evaluate and consider the possible answer. Questions cause the reader to have doubts, perhaps, about the truth or reliability of the information that is being presented. They enable the writer to express their doubts about a subject matter, e.g. *Why did she leave? Where did she go? What was the reason?*
>
> **A rhetorical question** is a particular kind of question designed to directly involve the audience; to make the reader take a moment to consider their own stance (and whether it is the same as the writer), e.g. *Have you ever thought about donating to charity?*

1 Choose **one** question from the text. Explain the effect and the purpose of the question. Here is an example.

'Is it hot enough for you yet?' This is a rhetorical question and the effect is challenging the reader personally to consider how much heat is comfortable. The purpose of the question (because it is the title of the piece) is to prime us to consider how much we are willing to endure/put up with the heating up of our planet until it is too hot – for us as well as all living things. We expect the essay to contain the writer's answer and should be interested to compare how similar (or different) it is to our own.

_____

_____

_____

_____

_____

> **An assertion** is a declaration of a strongly held idea or opinion, often without evidence provided to back up the statement, e.g. *Teenagers are the worst age group to parent.* A clever writer can be persuasive and convincing if they are able to slip in an assertion amongst statements they validate with statistics or quoting authority.

2 Choose **one** assertion from the text. Explain the effect and the purpose of the assertion. Here is an example.

'But doing nothing doesn't mean that things will stay as they are.' Slack has just finished discussing the arguments by a range of non-experts why nothing can be done to stop climate change. By starting his assertion with the word 'But' he is giving a rebuttal to that thinking. He now asserts one of his key concerns: things are going to get worse even if we refuse to change the actions which are causing harm to the planet. The assertion is a warning and the purpose is to pull the reader towards the evidence he then provides in the hope, perhaps, that we will indeed do something because, 'yes, it is too hot for us now.'

_____

_____

_____

_____

_____

Putting it together

QUESTION ONE

Examine the way the writer emphasises his concern about the planet, referring to at least TWO specific aspects of written text.

Aspects may include parallel construction, quoting, imperative, questions.

You should start your answer using the words of the question. If you are stuck, you can use some of the sentence starters on pages 98 and 108.

If you require more space to complete your answer, please move on to your own paper and attach it to this page.

POEM: *Me, the Labourer* by Eti Sa'aga

Reading the text

Read the poem, out loud if possible. And then read it again making any annotations that come instinctively to you: question marks, words/images which stand out, etc.

Me, the Labourer

Me,
the labourer, sweat
in the sun,
to pave the road
5   for the richman
to ride on in comfort.
My friend is the wind
is cool on my body,
and the sun
10   is warm my soul
from the stares and frowns
of the people who pass
me by.
They don't like me
15   but they don't say it
because they need me
to do their dirty work.

I does my work hard
and think of me.
20   Is good to have me
think of me
for there's no one to
think of me but me.
My wife and kids
25   think I'm very good worker
but I get very little money.
The road is finished
and pretty speeches are said.
The richman rides ahead,
30   satisfied.
More cars go by
and race on into the evening.
But silently
on the roadside
35   I stand.
No one sees me.
No one waves.
No one remembers me
for the road I made.
40   I walk back
to the warmth of
my wife and family.
When is it to be
my day?

Eti Sa'aga

Immediate response

1 Use the space below to record your first impressions. You can jot down singular words, phrases and/or ideas.

2 What aspect of the text did you most engage with? What will you remember?

3 What does it make *you* think about?

4 How would different people view this poem differently (dependent on gender, age, ethnic background, worldview, etc.)?

Unpacking the text

1 IDENTIFYING THE TONE

a What types of feelings and atmosphere does this piece create for you?

b Reread the text and:
   i Highlight, using differing colours, positive and negative words and phrases.
   ii Organise the positive and negative words and phrases into two lists.

Positive	Negative

iii Look at the words listed on the previous page. Describe the tone of the poem. Do not use the words 'positive' or 'negative'. Be more specific, e.g. 'resentful', 'hopeful', 'nervous', 'funny'.

The tone is mostly _____ because of words such as _____

_____

_____.

c Identify the main subject/topic of the poem.

_____

d Write down a quote that describes (or shows) the subject.

_____

_____

e Describe the writer's attitude to the subject. Use examples from the poem to support your answer.

The writer is _____ because

he uses words like _____ when describing

_____.

These words make the reader think about _____

_____ because _____

_____

_____.

Identifying the 'point of change'

All fiction (poetry and narrative prose) has a 'point of change' in it. The point of change shows us the writer's **attitude** towards the subject, which helps us understand the writer's purpose. Identifying and understanding the point of change is a strategy used to analyse the poem.

1 Identify the line where the point of change occurs. _____

2 Describe the atmosphere before this change. _____

_____

3 Identify two words that contribute to this atmosphere.

a _____ **b** _____

4 Describe what the atmosphere is after the change.

_____

Identifying and discussing the effects of how the poem is communicated

1   The following **language features/techniques** can be found in the poem. Find and label on the text (on page 121) an example of each of the techniques in the box below. Refer to the glossary (at the back of the book) if you do not know these words.

> personal pronoun   imagery   cliché   repetition
> alliteration   personification   contrast

2   Complete the following grid of **language features/techniques**. We have done some of it for you and provided space for you to add one of your own. You could continue this grid on your own paper and attach here. 📎

Technique	Example(s)	Effect	Why it is effective	How does this develop our understanding of the writer's purpose?
Imagery	'pave the road'			
Repetition	'think of me'	Brings the reader back again to what the narrator wants us to do.		
	I me my		These remind us that this account is through the eyes of the labourer and so is his perspective.	

Language focus: Diction

Diction is the word choice or the writing style of the author. These choices help to suggest tone: e.g. formal, informal, uneducated, sophisticated, wealthy, foreign, etc.

The four main ways diction is used:

- **to create a certain tone that supports the purpose.** Compare, for example, the words used in a short story by Katherine Mansfield with those words used in a scientific paper or a Year 13 Biology textbook.

- **to support the setting.** The writer uses words and language associated with the time and place and the cultural concerns. 'Colloquial diction' is when a writer has their characters speak the language native to that time and place. Examples of this can be seen in works by Charles Dickens and Jane Austen.

- **to establish a narrative voice and tone.** The diction of a piece helps the reader understand the writer's attitude towards the subject of their text.

- **to bring characters to life.** Through dialogue especially we can tell a lot about a character's personality and the details of their background.

1 Discuss the diction of two of the examples from the poem. Explain the effect and the purpose of the example.
- 'richman'
- 'I does my work hard'
- 'Is good to have me / think of me'
- 'think I'm very good worker'

_____

_____

_____

_____

_____

_____

_____

_____

_____

_____

_____

_____

_____

_____

_____

_____

_____

Putting it together

QUESTION TWO

Discuss the way in which the poet develops a sympathetic narrative voice in the poem, referring to at least TWO specific aspects of written text.

Aspects may include imagery, cliché, repetition, diction.

If you require more space to complete your answer, please move on to your own paper and attach it to this page.

COMPARING TEXTS

To prepare for this answer, plan your response on some extra paper, using the steps and Venn diagrams on pages 110 and 111 as a guide.

QUESTION THREE
Compare how the writers develop a distinctive tone, referring to at least ONE specific aspect used in each text.

Aspects may include repetition, imperative, diction, rhetorical question.

_____

_____

_____

_____

_____

_____

_____

_____

_____

_____

_____

_____

_____

_____

_____

_____

_____

_____

_____

_____

_____

_____

_____

_____

_____

_____

_____

_____

_____

_____

_____

_____

_____

_____

If you require more space to complete your answer, please move on to your own paper and attach it to this page.

SET 3

Now that you have completed the activities on the first four texts, you are ready to attempt a set as if you were under exam conditions. Using all of the skills you have been practising throughout this section, give the following questions your best shot. For each one put your timer on for 20 minutes. Read the piece and use your strategies to answer the question. Good luck!

PROSE: *Myself, Looking Back* by Grahame Sydney

Myself, Looking Back

On the wall above my side of our bed at Cambrian Road there is a framed drawing of Donald Duck, a portrait really – head and neck only – with a fence and poplar trees in the background. Donald Duck in New Zealand, looking a little deranged. Crayon on creased, brown paper, one large corner of which has been torn off. The artist evidently felt some pride in this effect, wished to be identified: it has a signature at the bottom that reads G. Sydney 1957.

I can clearly remember doing this drawing. I am nine years old, sitting at the varnished wood table in the dining room, my stubby school crayons, fat as thumbs, all scattered to my right, and sheets of fresh newsprint littering the tabletop. In front of me the red corrugated iron roof of Jess and Harry Rolls's house next door almost fills one window frame. The place is only a few metres away from ours, with a scrawny hedge jammed between them. Past the settee to my right, another large picture window looks over a long backyard and Dad's veg garden, across the colourful patchwork of Kew neighbourhood roofs down to the St Clair flats where Mum was born, the long stretch of St Clair and Saint Kilda beaches with their constant margin of white, foaming surf, and the cold blue horizon of the Pacific Ocean.

As always, the sea is flecked with white-caps, whipped by an irascible southerly, in the flat and black pyramid of brave little White Island, raw rock with a spattered cap of gull dung, is once again being thrashed by bullying breakers. We all know that over the faraway horizon lies South America. Behind my back the fire is spitting away, so it is probably winter. Presumably a weekend, or after school perhaps – too raw to be outside. In another corner the radiogram is on 4ZB, a constant murmur. I am by myself in the room, doing my drawings. Finished ones are on the floor. Mum is in the kitchen: I can hear her through the small open slide that joins the two rooms, pottering about, doing whatever it is she does all day – plates and bowls and tins, and the occasional bang of the oven door.

It's no surprise this Donald Duck has survived fifty-six years, despite its fragility. My mother kept everything I did. When she died I inherited an assortment of cardboard boxes, all tied with ribbons of discarded nylon stockings, plus a deep, ruptured suitcase, every one of them filled to capacity with the scraps of my early years, and evidence of her devotional admiration for everything I produced. Unaware at the time she was holding these trivial things, I look at them now with some fascination and discomfort.

The fascination comes with being able to remember almost every single one, where I was when I drew them, what was happening around me and what I thought. The same still applies today: each painting is a vault of infested memory, instantly conjuring recollections of the private, sometimes secret place from which they grew, as well is the more obvious public associations.

(...) My discomfort, on inspecting these preserved and inconsequential scribblings, arises because I see in them no sign at all of natural ability or precociousness; they contain no clue of the 'talent' my mother believed to be such 'a gift'. I argued with her years later about such misguided notions, but despite somewhat crude derision from my unshakable atheist corner she held stubbornly to these convictions. It was a mother's blind love. There is no suggestion of anything special in those juvenile things, aside from – in their abundance – my own curious dedication to the business, and the prolific, possibly obsessive output.

But most children draw, easily losing themselves in the entertainment of colours and lines. Kids colour in, paint and then invent stories to explain the puzzling, often obscure and wild graphics; my own immersion in that fantasy world was no different from every other neighbourhood child, save perhaps that urge to produce more, and the constant encouragement I received to do so.

Grahame Sydney

QUESTION ONE

Discuss the way in which the writer explores the early evidence of his skill as an artist, referring to at least TWO specific aspects of written text.

Aspects may include allusion, anecdote, personification, alliteration.

_____

_____

_____

_____

_____

_____

_____

_____

_____

_____

_____

_____

_____

_____

_____

_____

_____

_____

_____

_____

_____

_____

_____

_____

If you require more space to complete your answer, please move on to your own paper and attach it to this page.

POEM: *It's taken me all morning for her to do this*
by Nicola Easthope

It's taken me all morning for her to do this

She is nearly ten
she is made of fat books and travels inside herself
she is her own time machine.

She has made one of three party invites —
5   the first is neat and stickerful,
the other two are not made yet

and probably won't be unless I threaten her
with a fat book ban. She has pushed buttons
to go back in time, off to play with furry, fanged things.

10   Her time machine crashes into the Pleistocene.
She plays all the parts, answering the audience of her —
      It is wondrous to be here at this theatre!

      Oh my goodness, Commence!
She is good at posh British accents —
15   *Lovely, lovely to see everybody!*

      You may kiss the Smilodon!
      His lips were a custard pie —
which reminds me of the best ever pashes

in kitchens, during winter-hot desserts,
20   that she will not know about for years
and years. O, girl beyond atlases and clocks,

birthday girl with inky fingers,
see you at the i-list robosaur dance parties
long after the long tail of the Anthropocene.

                       Nicola Easthope

QUESTION TWO
Discuss the way in which the writer characterises her daughter, referring to at least TWO specific aspects of written text.

Aspects may include metaphor, repetition, allusion, personal pronoun.

_____

_____

_____

COMPARING TEXTS

To prepare for this answer, plan your response on some extra paper, using the steps and Venn diagrams on pages 110 and 111 as a guide.

QUESTION THREE

Compare how the writers show the way mothers respond to their children's abilities, referring to at least ONE specific aspect used in each text.

Aspects may include adjectives, metaphor, direct address, imagery.

GLOSSARY

TERM	DEFINITION	EXAMPLE
abridged	When you shorten a text (book, film, poem) without losing the main sense of it.	
adjective	Describing word; describes the noun.	hot, cold, blue, big, small
adverb	Describing word; describes the verb (how or when or where the action is done).	he smiled **sadly** they were **nowhere** **Yesterday**, I went to the park.
alliteration	The repetition of consonant sounds.	**T**iny **T**im **t**rod on **D**on's **t**oes. (The 'd' is also alliteration.)
allusion	A reference to another literary or well-known work.	I was no **Shakespeare** but I loved writing plays.
analyse	To understand the whole of the text better by identifying the individual parts, how and why they work the way they do and the combined effect of them.	
anecdote	A story used to illustrate an idea.	When I was a small child …
assertion	A declaration of a strongly held idea or opinion, often without evidence provided to back up the statement.	Teenagers are the worst age group to parent.
assonance	The deliberate repetition of the same vowel sound followed by a different consonant sound.	A st**i**tch **i**n t**i**me saves n**i**ne.
book ending	Phrases and/or ideas which are placed at the beginning and at the end of a passage.	
cliché	An over-used expression.	It was a dark and stormy night.
colloquialism	Informal language, usually spoken.	Howzit going, bro?
compound word	Two or more words are joined together to form a new word; sometimes joined with a hyphen - .	babysitter, mother-in-law, homegrown
conjunction	A word that joins two sentences together.	and, but, so
contrast	The use of words or images which are opposite in likeness.	I was feeling **hot** and **cold** all night.
convincing	Including more than one example to support what you are saying and explain what you mean.	
dash	(–) Used to set apart a word or a phrase.	– hand / out and greeting –
diction	The word choice or the writing style of the author. These choices help to suggest tone: e.g. formal, informal, uneducated, sophisticated, etc.	*'therefore, ye soft pipes, play on …'* the use of the formal 'ye' instead of the informal 'you' shows the respect the urn inspires in Keats.
euphemism	A nicer way of saying something that is usually unpleasant or unkind.	He was 'let got' (fired). She's under the weather (sick).
extended metaphor	A comparison using a metaphor is used and then the comparisons are further added to.	
facts/statistics	Numbers and specific examples used to support an argument.	65% of statistics are made up. She's worked here for 18 years so knows what is going on.

  ISBN: 978017045445

TERM	DEFINITION	EXAMPLE
fiction	Made-up story to entertain, persuade and/or teach a moral.	
hyperbole	An exaggeration.	I'm so tired I could sleep for a month.
hyphenated words	Words joined by a hyphen to indicate they have a combined meaning or that they are linked in some way.	pick-me-up, short-term
imagery	Used to communicate visually an idea and/or create a mood.	
imperative/command	An order or command of an action.	Don't hit your sister.
incomplete sentence	A sentence without a verb and/or subject.	Unfortunately for them. After the rain.
infer	Hint; imply; suggest.	
irony	The message intended is different (usually opposite) to the literal meaning of words used. Most common are sarcasm and understatement.	Sarcasm: Yeah, we're doing *a great job* of looking after the plant. Understatement: Might be *a bit warm* living near the equator.
jargon	Specialised language used by people who work together or share a common interest.	Getting **endorsement** for all **subjects** is good but you still need to have **Level 2 Literacy** for **University Entrance**.
juxtaposition	The deliberate placing of two things side by side by comparison or contrast.	We invited both our **friends** and our **enemies**.
listing	Related words or phrases arranged as a list.	I eat toast, cereal, and a banana for breakfast.
metaphor	A comparison between two things where one thing is said to be another.	The playground **is a jungle** and all the students **are wild animals**.
minor sentence	Word, phrase or clause similar to a sentence but lacking completeness of a full sentence.	The whole smell and taste of him.
narrator	The person or character who is telling the version of events/story.	
non-fiction	A piece of writing based on facts and reality or offering an opinion.	biography, autobiography, textbook, letter to the editor, speech
onomatopoeia	The sound of the word imitates or suggests the meaning or noise of the action described.	crash, gurgle
oxymoron	When two opposite ideas are joined together.	A cruel kindness.
parallel construction/structure	Repeating the same word class order in close succession, e.g. proper noun + adjective + verb + preposition + noun.	'It was the best of times, it was the worst of times, ...' (Charles Dickens, *A Tale of Two Cities*)
parenthesis	Inserted into a sentence as an explanation or afterthought, usually marked by brackets, dashes, or commas.	My father, the one in the red hat, loves to dress up. Take the water (250 ml) and add to the flour.
past tense	When verb forms show that the time/action has already been.	walked; loved
perceptive	Making links between the ideas in the text and your observation of the wider contexts (either the fictional world of the text or the real world).	
personal pronoun	A word that stands in place of a proper noun.	he, she, me, you, I, we, us, them, they

TERM	DEFINITION	EXAMPLE
personification	When a non-living thing is given living characteristics or when a non-human thing is given human characteristics.	The **lift groaned** on the way down.
possessive pronoun	Word that indicates ownership.	my, mine, our, his, yours
preposition	Word used to show the position of a thing in relation to another thing.	on, above, behind, inside, under
present tense	When verb forms show that the time/action is happening now.	she opens up / his drawer and takes out / his favourite shirt.
proper noun	A noun that refers to a specific person, place, object, or period of time.	Mr Jones; Hamilton; National Heart Foundation
pun	An expression that plays on different meanings of the same word or phrase.	I've been to the dentist so many times, I know the drill.
punctuation	The marks used in writing sentences to clarify meaning, e.g. comma, full stop, capital letter, question mark, etc.	
quotation	Direct use of another's words either spoken or written.	As the principal reminds us, 'To lead, you must serve.'
repetition	Words or statements used more than once for effect.	The room was **cold**. Too **cold** to think.
rhetorical question	A question to which no answer is required (to involve the audience).	Have you ever thought about donating to charity?
rhyme	The repetition of words with similar sounds.	There was an old horse from Cant**ucket** who ate from a rusted brown b**ucket**.
rhythm	The beat or pattern of stresses that occurs in poetry and music and often used for effect in prose.	
short sentences	One- to three-word sentences, often phrases.	Try it. Now.
show understanding	Explain your statements in terms of the meanings and effects created.	
sibilance	Repetition of 's' sounds in two or more words. Often used to indicate a sinister event or feeling.	The **s**lippery **s**nake **s**lithered acro**ss** the gra**ss**.
simile	A phrase that compares two things, using 'like', 'as' or 'than'.	They behave **like** monkeys in the classroom but are **as well behaved as** royalty in the playground.
structure	How the story/text starts: first word, first sentence, first detail and/or action. Which characters are introduced and in which order. How the story ends: last event, last sentence, last word. Where the critical moment or climax is in the text. The order of the events/narration, e.g. linear (the story unfolds chronologically), flash forwards/flashbacks, etc.	
symbol	An image/picture which represents an idea.	Dove represents peace.
tone	The overall impression of the author's attitude towards a topic, event, or character.	Humorous, sad, happy, peaceful
use of punctuation	The deliberate use of the comma or exclamation mark or ellipsis or other punctuation marks for effect.	
use of te reo Māori	Using Māori words, expression – often without immediate translation.	**Kia ora**, friends, I send my **aroha** to you.
verb	A doing word.	I **ate** my lunch then **walked** to class.

SELECTED ANSWERS

You will find some sample answers to selected activities here. Many of the questions do not have one correct response so if you get a different answer to us, don't assume you are wrong. Think about why we wrote that answer and why you wrote your answer. Talk to someone else about their answer. Discussing how and why you came to a response is another excellent skill to learning how to get familiar with unfamiliar texts. Most of the time in English analysis, provided you can support it with clear examples and explanations, your answer is correct for your reading of the text.

Due to limitations of space we have not provided answers to the language features/techniques grids or the long, essay-styled answers here, however these can be found on our website by searching the name of this book or by typing the following link into your browser: https://cengage.co.nz/GFWUF3_Long_Answers.

Chapter One: PLACES

SET 1

PROSE: *Philosophy from a kayak on a summer's evening* by Grant Shimmin (pages 5–15)

Pre-reading activities (pages 5–6)

1 PREDICTING

   a Some suggestions:

      Peaceful; beautiful; authentic; space and time to think about things that everyday life doesn't allow you the time to consider; big ideas considered (use of the word philosophy).

   b Possibly more playful but the fact it says philosophy makes me think it will be reflective and consider some of the big issues that were prevalent at the start of 2020 (bushfires in Australia, climate change, etc.).

2 VOCABULARY WORK

   a

obscured	Not clear or plain; ambiguous, vague, or uncertain.
celestial	Pertaining to the sky or visible heaven.
sparse	Small in number or amount and spread out over an area.
rendezvous	To meet up with someone, often secretly.
postured politicians	Pretending to have a particular opinon or attitude.
vested	Fixed; settled; absolute.
Stoicism	Philosophy which teaches self-control when faced with hardship.
mahi	Te reo Māori word for work.

   b Some suggestions; get a friend or teacher to check yours.

     i The trees were so <u>sparse</u> we could see up into the <u>celestial</u> realms of the night sky.

     ii She was oblivious to the <u>mahi</u> her husband did around the house and instead maintained her own sense of <u>stoicism</u>.

     iii They wanted to <u>rendezvous</u> sooner so that they could get the best spot where their view was not <u>obscured</u>.

Immediate response (page 8)

These are your personal responses to the work and, as such, we have not listed the answers as there will be many different responses.

Post-reading questions (page 9)

1 He shows us a world where there is a lot of bad happening but that there are a lot of people and organisations who are doing really good things and that this somehow cancels out the bad. In fact, it offers hope that the world can become a better place despite all the bad things which afflict our planet. 'the onslaught of negativity and hopelessness isn't all there is. There is still kindness in the world, compassion, empathy, from many ordinary people, who do what they can where they are and make life better for others, maybe a few, maybe many, but they persist, shining through the gaps in the global gloom cloud.'

2 Because being outside in nature, away from the routines of home/work/life, allows your mind to wander and for you to consider things you don't normally have the space and time to think about. Being out in nature, virtually alone, 'sparse evening crowd', watching a beautiful sunset, 'some sort of celestial royal flush', allowed Shimmin to contemplate that the world is a beautiful place, even though lots of bad things are happening right now, 'it was tough not to feel down about the future of the human race' and that all of us can do something to help counteract the bad, 'if only each of us … had a vision of what is in our power to do.'

Unpacking the text (pages 9–11)

1 THE TITLE UNLOCKED

   a **Literal**: thinking, a single-person small-boat, the time of summer when it's hot, in the early evening.

     Figurative: being on your own and considering the big questions/answers at a time after ('evening') the best time of one's life (summer) or a time when there has been a lot of light (summer has long days) and things have been hot – which often makes things uncomfortable if it's too hot. This is the time when we often consider the deeper/harder issues when we are alone and in a position of possible danger (kayaking).

   b *Philosophy from a kayak on a summer's evening means* thinking while kayaking in the evening of summer time *and also means* thinking about important issues to do with life after a time of being in the heat and light.

     This is an appropriate title for the first extract because the author was already wondering if it was a good idea that they were doing this activity so questioning himself. It's not until he's out on the water that he comes to understand an important idea which he wouldn't have gained if he'd been distracted by the busyness of life. He realises that, in the quietness of his time on the water, there ARE places of peace and therefore he CAN find a place amongst the chaos of the world to find peace. He will just have to make an effort, like making the effort to go out kayaking.

   c Answers will vary.

2 IDENTIFYING THE TONE

   a Answers will vary.

   b **ii** **Positive**: raised; calm; inviting; I'd forgotten that; celestial flush; paid off; start of the pay-out; show; warm evening sunshine; birdsong; peace; contentment; extraordinary; calmer; optimism; greeted the dawn; haven; stunning; reminded; kindness; compassion; empathy; persist; shining; courageous; concentrate; within your power;

disregard the hysteria; in your power; lucky; boost; spreading kindness; empowering others; just try to stop them; vision; power; sun; turning the water to molten gold.
Negative: wasted; direct impact; obscured; briefly struck me; eerie accompaniment; bushfire smoke; obliterated; sepia tone; fires raged; fighting for their homes and their lives; politicians postured; fouled the air; stench; assassination; reprisal; missile strike; been on my mind; despite; bemoaning; world was … going to hell; tough; feel down; future of the human race; obliviousness; disinformation; discernment; onslaught; negativity; hopelessness; gaps; global gloom cloud; struggling people.

    iii *The tone is mostly* hopeful *and* positive *because of words such as* 'contentment, stunning, reminded and power.'

c The main topic of this text is how things may seem overwhelming at the moment with all of the negative things going on, but we can make a difference, one person at a time.

d 'It was tough not to feel down about the future of the human race … but this, spreading kindness, empowering others … a vision of what is in our power to do.'

e *The writer is* ultimately optimistic about things *because he uses words like* 'contentment', 'peace', 'empathy', 'compassion', 'kindness' *when describing* how he is reminded that, despite all the bad things happening in the world, there are still lots of people doing good which kind of cancels out the bad. *These words make the reader think* about the gentleness of people and the positive attributes and acts of people *because* the writer had just spent some time discussing the bad events that are happening in the world but the time of the water calmed him down and gave him an opportunity to not only notice the loveliness of being on the water but thinking about the loveliness of people.

3 FIND THE PATTERN

a The piece starts off slightly negative, with Shimmin wondering if it was silly to go out kayaking so late. Then we have a series of positive descriptions of where he is and then how he is feeling. This leads into a section of negativity, where Shimmin describes how the year started with NZ having the 'eerie accompaniment of Australian bushfire smoke that obliterated the evening sun'. He then goes on to talk about the American assassination and retaliation from Iran via a missile strike. However, this is followed up by a series of positive words and overwhelmingly, the piece finishes with positive words about how as individuals we can make a difference and enjoy being in this world.

b *The writer wants us to understand that* yes, the 'future of the human race' is 'tough not to feel down about' but that there is still beauty in the world *because* he doesn't want us to feel hopeless. *It's important we understand this truth because* it is easy to get overwhelmed in this world of negativity and 'disregard the hysteria and wrongness around you.'

Language focus: Passive/active voice (page 13)

1 a Subject = 'I'; passive voice
b Subject = 'the water'; active voice
c Subject = 'my spirits'; passive voice
d Subject = David Slack; active voice

2 Some suggestions:
a I found myself stopping occasionally as I headed back to rendezvous with him
b Calm and inviting was the water.
c My spirits were raised as we rounded the bend that offered the last sweeping view of Cass Bay before the road descended.
d Reminding us days earlier, column-writing gem that he is, David Slack …

POEM: *Ferry Road* by Mary McCallum (pages 16–24)

Pre-reading activities (page 16)

1 PREDICTING

a Ferry is a passenger ship. Road is something on land to get from one place to another easily.
Bit of an oxymoron to have the two placed together. Does it mean a shipping lane? Or does it mean a road that was used to 'ferry' people from one place to another?

b Carrying people; the Picton Ferry; holidays; water; trips; travelling.

c i Ferry Road.
  ii To be ahead of cars on the road, to be ahead of other walkers, perhaps it is a race?
  iii A red flowering tree often found in NZ. This is a te reo Māori word so it gives us the clue that this piece is set in NZ.
  iv Oxymoron is two opposite qualities – furious usually means really angry or sometimes can be a furious energy, doing something with lots of energy/power because you are mad. This doesn't seem to go with 'hope' which is usually a calm word which is very positive and optimistic – forward focused. Furious hope could mean that these people were determined to be hopeful in their journey to a new world (disembarking is the clue for this at this stage).
  v Answers will vary.

Immediate response (page 18)

These are your personal responses to the work and, as such, we have not listed the answers as there will be many different responses.

Unpacking the text (pages 18–19)

1 IDENTIFYING THE TONE

a Answers will vary.
b ii **Positive:** splashes; confetti; smiling; greeting; still we climb; celebration; jostle; hope; breathe.
    Negative: how fast we walk; spindly things; knitted cobwebs; blasted tree; crinkled; jostle; furious.
  iii *The tone is mostly* observational *because of words such as* 'we watch' *and* 'we turn to see'.

c The walk and the weather.
d 'How fast we walk', 'minds on each fast foot', 'we three breathe', 'watch / the weather coming in', 'All the weather'.
e *The writer is* observant *because she uses words like* 'newly grown spindly things' when describing the plants she can see on her walk. *These words make the reader think about* paying more attention to small details when they are outside *because* McCallum wants us to understand that the natural world holds so much wonder, if only you take the time to notice them.

Summarise (page 19)

1 The poem is about completing a walk amongst nature, trying to work within nature (beating the weather), noticing nature ('spindly things', 'blasted tree') and being aware of the history of a place ('the pā of Te Hiha once stood'). The poem is about being present and aware.

2 *The poet wanted to teach us about* being present and aware of where we are *because* it is important to realise that even if you think you are alone you are accompanied by nature (the weather in this case) and the ghosts of those that have gone before.

Identifying the 'point of change' (page 20)

1 Line 23.
2 Anxious, narrator is trying to complete the walk and beat the weather. Things that are noticed on the walk are 'growing spindly … cobwebs' and 'splashes of rātā' (red, like blood) which all have negative connotations, everything is written in one sentence up until this point.

3 Suggestions: spindly, cobwebs.
4 Positive and friendly: 'water crinkled as if smiling', 'hand out and greeting'.

Language focus: Rhythm (page 22)

1 The stress of the words 'from the heads – and by ... and how fast we walk/to be ahead' as if the poem is walking step by step up the hill — breaking out at 'weather' which deliberately throws you down to the weather creeping in, and then some two-syllable words.

2 Strong metre with 'each fast footfall' to show they are speeding up and hard on their heels is the weather — also quick (with its double meaning of fast and alive) — and with the repetition of 'breathe and breathe and breathe' they are speeding up too and tired but this also reminds them that there are three of them alive there. The weather is like a creature, chasing them. And the reader doesn't know at the end who wins.

3 The poem is one long sentence for that first part as they climb, stopping (at a full stop) when they stop to look down. And then at the lines 21 on, they start again with the antagonist in the poem: weather coming in and dogging them and then chasing them up that hill.

4 To show the looking — there's this and this and this. So that is a turning point syntactically and in terms of what is happening in the poem. Literally they stop and turn and look. Then comes a moment of reflecting on the stuff they don't see — the ghosts. So not so alone after all. Then the poem reduces down again at the end to two people and a dog who are alive and physical. Who breathe.

5 The personification of the wharf as it is like that, sticking out into a harbour calling people in, welcoming them, a haven after a rough ferry crossing.

SET 2

PROSE: *The Wrong One* by Chiao Lin (pages 29–35)

Immediate response (pages 30–31)
These are your personal responses to the work and, as such, we have not listed the answers as there will be many different responses.

Post-reading questions (pages 31–32)
1 a Poor
  b '... the cuff ... was fraying', 'Anna needs the shirt after you grow out of it.'
2 'They got the afternoon off school', '... if it had been Leah ... Lily would have stepped right over', 'but she couldn't ... they were boys', 'they could walk over her as they liked but her turn had never been and would never come'.
3 I think Anna steals the money so that she and Leah can buy pork buns instead of getting vegetable buns. Her crying and saying 'it's not fair' makes me sad because a girl that is young (five years younger than Lily) knows that boys are treated better than girls.
4 a Her male (younger) cousins.
  b The pork bun instead of the vegetable bun.
  c Because they are more expensive than a vegetable bun and because she is a girl, it appears that girls aren't as important as boys.
5 Lily is trying to convince herself that the bun is lovely and a treat, that it doesn't matter that it isn't the more expensive treat that her male cousins got.
  Answers to the second part of the question will vary.

Unpacking the text (page 32)
1 **IDENTIFYING THE TONE**
  a Answers will vary.
  b ii **Positive**: afternoon off; easy as pie; treats; lessened; chance; helped; beamed; thank you; smooth and flawless; real treat; aroma; sweetness; love it.

Negative: were in the way; jostling; tumbling; would've; couldn't; walk over her; never come; couldn't understand; told fibs; hastily; fiddled with the cuff; stop it; flushed; heart thumped; painfully; tears starting to form; but it's not fair; grabbed; ran; knot; one held responsible; beamed; tattered; always got what they wanted; scared.
  iii Answers will vary but tone could be: wistful; bewildered; angry; confused; resigned. Any quotes from the list above can be used to back up the tone selection.
  c The main subject of the text is about how males get treated better than females and how as a female, Lily is trying to convince herself that it doesn't actually matter. The title 'The Wrong One' probably doesn't actually mean the fact that Lily got a vegetable bun instead of a pork bun, but rather the fact she was born a girl instead of a boy.
  d This is one example only: 'They could walk over her as they liked, but her turn had never been and would never come.'
  e *The writer is* frustrated by how boys are treated better than girls *because she uses words like* 'they could walk over her as they liked, but her turn ... would never come' *when describing* how the male and female cousins interact. *These words make the reader think about* how we treat males and females in our society. This is important *because* we should be inclusive of all people and not discriminate on any grounds.

Language focus: Repetition (page 34)
1 a Epistrophe
  b It mimics the anticipation, hope, expectation that Lily has that she might get the prized bun with the red dot – a symbol of her importance (ironic given that the story highlights that as a girl she is less than the boys). It also serves to emphasise the disappointment when she gets the bun without the red spot.

POEM: *Mother* by Renee Liang (pages 36–41)

Immediate response (page 37)
These are your personal responses to the work and, as such, we have not listed the answers as there will be many different responses.

Unpacking the text (page 38)
1 **IDENTIFYING THE TONE**
  a Answers will vary.
  b ii **Positive**: raised; showed; wedding ring; shiny; holding her; learning; wag; new; runs; high-chair; opens.
    Negative: for others first; she's far; unfamiliar island; three cups for five mouths; last to sit down; words she's never heard; ask to explain; challenges; broken; discarded; until 10pm; wants; words boil; kill flies; after thirty seven years; empty beds; faded floral.
  iii *The tone is mostly* matter-of-fact *because of words such as* 'showed ... how to cook for others first' and 'pays for music lessons / buys a cake to take'.
  c The main subject of the poem is how women, particularly homemakers, put others before themselves and added to that, the difficulty of doing this in a country other than where you grew up.
  d 'she measures / the rice / three cups / for five mouths ... she's last / to sit down / at table.'
  e *The writer is* matter-of-fact/aware of the challenges of being a homemaker in another culture *because she uses words like* 'lays chopsticks on white plates' *when describing* setting the dining table and 'her children come home with words she's never heard'. *These words make the reader think about* the challenges of moving to another country with a foreign language *because* they point out how the narrator is trying to merge the two cultures together.

A closer look at the structure (page 39)
Answers will vary; get a friend or teacher to check yours.

Language focus: Imagery – Simile (page 41)
1 'her words boil like soup'
2 Can be hot, nourishing, sometimes words can come out in a rush if put under pressure, lots of ingredients, etc.
3 Soup is given often when someone is sick but if you don't watch it, it could boil over and burn on the stove; could be too hot for someone to swallow. Because the mother is angry with the way her husband is speaking to her, it feels like she has inside of her things to say which she would like to come out. Instead, she swallows the words in the same way she might swallow down soup that is too hot or not tasty.

Chapter Two: PEOPLE

SET 1

PROSE: *How We Fell* by Glenn Colquhoun (pages 49–57)

Pre-reading activities (page 49)
1 Answers will vary; get a friend or teacher to check yours.

Immediate response (page 50)
These are your personal responses to the work and, as such, we have not listed the answers as there will be many different responses.

Unpacking the text (page 50–53)
1 THE TITLE UNLOCKED
  a The castle that we built
    Literal: castle: a fortified, high-walled residence, usually large and home to royalty; we: to mean oneself and at least one other person; built: constructed by assembling
    Figurative: castle: a place to go to when under siege to find protection; impenetrable; hard to overcome/destroy; built: was responsible to create from scratch requiring effort.
  b *How We Fell means* falling to the ground or an accident that happened (in the past), the way something happened to two or more people who fell *and also means* making a mistake, falling in love, getting tricked into something. *This is an appropriate title for the first extract because* the extract talks about the positive and negative consequences of falling in and out of love.
    The title of the second text, The castle that we built, refers to a fortified, high-walled residence, usually large and home to royalty assembled or constructed by the author and at least one other person *and also means* an impenetrable place to go to when under siege to find protection; hard to overcome/destroy; built: was responsible for creating from scratch requiring effort. *This is an appropriate title because* the writer describes the way in which they created their relationship and fortified themselves against the rest of the world.

2 IDENTIFYING THE TONE
  a ii **Positive**: love, remarkable, purple, soft reliable, living, promised, flowers, clean, laughing.
    Negative: didn't, fall, slowly, flat, brown, no, noisy, broken, mad, barked, scared, argue, dragons, unkempt, creaked, cramming, haunted.
    iii Answers will vary; get a friend or teacher to check yours.
  b Subject is an account of the way the writer's relationship started and ended.

c 'I didn't mean to fall out of love either.'
d *The writer is* giving us an account of how his relationship ended *because* he uses words like 'broken/scared/argue/haunted' *when describing* what was happening to them and around them as their relationship started to end. *These words make the reader think about* the negative side of a relationship *because* they are negative words and are associated with things broken and how people feel when they are unhappy because something bad has happened.

3 FIND THE PATTERN
a and b Answers will vary; get a friend or teacher to check yours.

Identifying and discussing the effects of how the passages are communicated (page 55)
2 a Starting the text with 'I' and close to the ending of the passage, the word 'ourselves' shows the shift of the focus of the passage where the writer is an individual and focusing on their own thoughts and then ending with a focus on the couple together as one unit.
  b That being in love made them a bit crazy; that being in love showed that the world looked strange/different/crazy.
  c The description of how her clothes look shows how untidy/wild she was but also that there was beauty there.

Language focus: Adverbs/adverbial phrases (page 55)
1 a–c Answers will vary; get a friend or teacher to check yours.

POEM: *Near Death Experience* by John Allison (pages 58–65)

Pre-reading activities (page 58)
PREDICTING
1 a A near-death encounter is defined as an event in which the individual could very easily die or be killed, or may have already been considered clinically dead, but nonetheless survives, and continues his or her physical life. Source: digitalcommons.nl.edu
  b Answers will vary.

Immediate response (page 59)
These are your personal responses to the work and, as such, we have not listed the answers as there will be many different responses.

Unpacking the text (pages 59–61)
1 THE TITLE UNLOCKED
  a **Literal**: an event where the individual could have very easily died or be killed.
    Figurative: an experience that feels like the end of something; feels like it would have changed you so completely that you are no longer the same.
  b *Near Death Experience means* an event where the individual could have very easily died or be killed *and also means* an experience that feels like the end of something. *This is an appropriate title for the poem because* the narrator is reminiscing about her partner who is no longer with her and she discusses how his leaving/dying was like a fire and she was a tree that was burned to ash from the experience (dying).

2 IDENTIFYING THE TONE
  a Answers will vary.
  b ii **Positive**: seeing him again; favourite; quick smile; chest … she laid her head; enfolding her; skin is gloved; carefully; easily.

 ISBN: 9780170454445

Negative: times like these; as though; forest fire; foliage dissolves; sheathed in flame; breath go out of here; ash; incandescent; sinking; sun is setting; again.

   iii *The tone is mostly* nostalgic *because of words such as* 'at times like these' and 'as though trying it / against him standing there' alongside 'for a long time she is seeing / him again'.

c The main subject of the poem is how the narrator is without her partner and how she misses him but then at the same time how the loss of him/his leaving/the deterioration of the relationship was like a forest fire that burned her to ash. She regularly reminisces like this as the word 'again' is repeated and the 'drawer ... slides shut so easily' which shows it is used a lot.

d 'for a long time she is seeing / him again', 'The whole smell and taste of him', 'She is a tree ... The foliage dissolves, / her limbs are sheathed in flame.' 'puts it back ... into his drawer.' 'slides shut so easily'

e *The writer is* recognising how the loss of someone you love can just about cause you to die *because he uses words like* 'seeing / him again' and 'her limbs are sheathed in flame' *when describing* the emotions she goes through while holding his favourite shirt out in front of her. *These words make the reader think about* the impact of death/loss on the people left behind *because* the poet compares her memories to a 'forest / fire' which turns her to 'sinking, ash.'

Identifying the 'point of change' (page 61)

1 Line 19.
2 Nostalgic, sad but also happy as she is remembering his 'quick smile' and their closeness; favourite; holds it; as though; long time; seeing him again; quick smile; laid her head; his arms enfolding; once familiar changes.
3 Grief stricken, broken.
4 Everything destroyed.

Summarise (page 61)

1 This poem is about a woman who is grieving the loss of her partner. She seeks comfort in his favourite shirt and it gives it briefly but then it brings up her grief which wracks her like a forest fire.
2 *The poet wanted to teach us about* the long-lasting effects of grief *because* often we assume that because people seem fine, they have moved on from their grief. The fact that the narrator 'puts it back / again' shows that she often completes this act – getting the favourite shirt out to remember her partner but then feeling like a tree consumed by fire. The title helps us be aware that for her, the loss of her partner has brought her 'near death' herself and that she will need on-going support.

Point of view (page 62)

1 By writing in third-person you can show both the characters' thoughts along with what is actually happening. By writing as a female experiencing grief, we are more likely to feel a sense of sympathy for her than a male as he is meant to be 'strong' and 'tough'. Allison runs a risk here though, because assuming a gender other than your own as a narrator has the possibility of the character ringing false (because the writer is writing as a female, of which they have no experience of being).

Identifying and discussing the effects of how the poem is communicated (page 62)

1 Metaphor: 'she is a tree'
    Listing: 'she is ash, incandescent, sinking, ash.'
    Adjective: 'favourite; quick; carefully'
    Possessive pronoun: 'his', 'her'

Use of present tense: 'at times like these', 'she is holding'
Minor sentence: 'the whole smell and taste of him.' 'Again.'
Repetition: 'she is', 'again'

Language focus: 'Present participle' and 'the gerund' (page 63)
Here is a list of the present participles. Get your teacher to check your explanation(s):
Unfolding, trying, seeing, enfolding, standing, sinking, setting

SET 2

PROSE: *The Writing Teacher* by T.K. Roxborogh (pages 70–76)

Immediate response (pages 71–72)
These are your personal responses to the work and, as such, we have not listed the answers as there will be many different responses.

Post-reading questions (page 72)
2 It is a key moment in history – many people remember the time.
3 Answers will vary. Some suggestions:
    disgusted: 'sour smell of booze'
    fun-loving: 'coming down the hill in the sledge with him in front'
4 Answers will vary.

Unpacking the text (page 73)
1 **IDENTIFYING THE TONE**
    a Answers will vary.
    b ii **Positive:** unwavering memory; happiness; not crying; warm; yellow with sunlight; happy; sunlight; laugh; without the sour smell of booze; picked me up; giggles; ticklish; bubbles; hushed; pleased; burnt bum (said with humour); shimmering; winked; pleased; included; naughtiness; sober; sweetest fella.
        Negative: don't believe; bare wooden floor; unfinished; brief; blurry; rare happiness; batted; argue; it's impossible; sent us away; strange; staccato; cold-blue; broken glass; blood; yelling; door shatter; crying; domestic abuse; unhappiness; shadowing; cry; dull; shadow; frost monster; crying; hospital; factory accident; told him off; leaves; beer; stroppy; maudlin; violent; rolled his car; shotgun; drunk in charge of a vehicle; drunk again; prison; waited; every day; alone; how long; cried; noise got switched off; suddenly quiet.
      iii *The tone is mostly* sad *because of such words as* 'unfinished', 'strange', 'crying', etc.
    c How and why she remembers the moon landing despite being a small child.
    d 'This moment is an unwavering memory because there was rare happiness in my house.'
    e *The writer is* defiant about her recollections of seeing the famous moon landing *because she uses words like* 'Bite me!' and 'I know what I know' *when describing* the details of what she remembers and an acknowledgement of what the experts might say. *These words make the reader think about* the impact of what goes through the mind of a child when they encounter significant events *because* even though the adults around them can tell them what happened, it's how the child feels at the time which seems to dictate how they remember things.

Language focus: Sentence types (page 75)
1 a subordinate clause
    b simple sentence (main clause)
    c compound sentence
    d complex sentence
2 Answers will vary; get a friend or teacher to check yours.

POEM: *My Father Today* by Sam Hunt (pages 77–82)

Immediate response (page 78)
These are your personal responses to the work and, as such, we have not listed the answers as there will be many different responses.

Unpacking the text (pages 78–79)
1   **IDENTIFYING THE TONE**
    b **ii** **Positive**: friends; met; my old man; Heaven; elegantly dressed; staring out to sea; wonders.
          Negative: buried; cold clay; heavy south wind towed … light away; dumb; lost for words; worlds away; last afternoon; staring out to sea; yelling; explode; buried him in clay; heavy load; dead father.
      iii Possible tone descriptors: bleak; gloomy; unenthusiastic; grief stricken; cold.
    c Main subject topic ideas: the poet's father has died and the poet is reflecting on what this loss means. How there is nothing to say. And yet he is being buried not in peace but where magpies are going to make a lot of noise.
    d 'They buried him today', 'There was nothing to say', 'I heard the bitchy chords', 'My old man, he's worlds / away', 'He was a heavy load, / my dead father today.'
    e *The writer is* grief-stricken *because he uses words like* 'My old man, he's worlds /away' *when describing* the burial of his father. *These words make the reader think about* the death of their own father and how permanent it is *because* the poet seems to feel a numb sense of loss.

Identifying and discussing the effects of how the poem is communicated (page 80)
1   Alliteration: '**c**old **c**lay'
    Imagery: 'They buried … my father in cold clay.', 'A heavy south wind towed / the drape of light away'
    Personification: 'A heavy south wind **towed** / the drape of light away'
    Adjectives: 'cold', 'heavy', 'bitchy'
    Proper nouns: 'Schnapper Rock Road', 'Heaven'
    Repetition: 'My old man', 'my father', 'old-man / pine', 'dead father'
    Parallel structure/book ending: 'They buried him today / up Schnapper Rock Road, / my father in cold clay' and 'up Schnapper Rock Road... / They buried him in clay. / He was a heavy load, / my dead father today.'

Language focus: Allusion (page 81)
Suggestions only.
1   **a** my father in cold clay: refers to the cold corpse of a person being buried and that God made man from the earth (clay); also references Chaucer's poem called 'Wake Wake Renowned Ghost From That Cold Clay.'
    b 'of magpies in an old-man / pine': referencing the Denis Glover poem *The Magpies* which represents an older time of farming as well as the birds being a nuisance.
    c He was a heavy load: to have responsibility for something heavy or difficult. Refers to beasts of burden (mules or donkeys) who traditionally carry things people are not able to.

Chapter Three: PROBLEMS AND POTENTIAL
SET 1
PROSE: *Whakamā* by Kirsty Dunn (pages 90–99)

Pre-reading activities (page 90)
1   Māori Dictionary: **1. (verb)** to be ashamed, shy, bashful, embarrassed.
2   Answers will vary.

Immediate response (page 92)
These are your personal responses to the work and, as such, we have not listed the answers as there will be many different responses.

Unpacking the text (pages 92–95)
1   **THE TITLE UNLOCKED**
    a **Literal:** means to be ashamed, shy, bashful, embarrassed.
        Figurative: it means not wanting to try, to feel useless,
    b *The word 'whakamā' means* to be ashamed, shy, bashful or embarrassed *and also means* not wanting to try or to feel useless. *This is an appropriate title for the piece because* Dunn is discussing when and why she has felt shame about her ability in te reo Māori. It is literally what the piece is about.

2   **IDENTIFYING THE TONE**
    b **ii** **Positive**: nicest; flurry of footsteps; we are cool; 'best student'; grateful; solidarity; confidence; to take steps; awe; knowledge; grateful; kindness; aroha; shares; beauty of whakapapa; knowledges and worldviews; our; our story is just a small part of a much bigger story.
          Negative: perpetually embarrassed; push each other; 'shame'; 'try hard' lacerates; beyond all recognition; trying hard; defiant; stares; challenging; 'said it wrong'; exhausted; overcome; embarrassment; stupid; reliving the shame; reimagine; shame is speaking and not being understood; not being able to understand; fluorescent lights; nowhere to hide; surges; limited; whakamā; hesitant; puku tighten; failed; not shown my gratitude; not put into practice; confront; stolen; physically punished; inherited silences; apprehensive; nervous; shocked.
      iii *The tone is mostly* that of anger and resentment *because of words such as* 'shame', 'embarrassed' *and* 'failed'.
    c The main subject/topic of this article is the whakamā Dunn feels at not knowing her own language.
    d For example 'Shame is speaking and not being understood'.
    e *The writer is* angry *because she uses words like* 'stupid', 'embarrassed' *and* 'ashamed' *when describing* her experiences with using (or not using) te reo Māori. *These words make the reader think about* how unfair and difficult this situation must be *because* the language was, as pointed out in the article, stolen from people like Dunn and they should never have been in this situation.

3   **FIND THE PATTERN**
    a Answers will vary; get a friend or teacher to check yours.
    b *The writer wants us to understand that* our words have the power to hurt *because* they can add to the shame we feel when we try to do something new. *It's important we understand this truth so that* we don't give up when we are finding things hard but also not to give someone else a hard time trying something like speaking te reo Māori if one does not feel skilled at it.

Suggestions only.

1 a thousand eyes: lots of people watching; judgement; being exposed; different points of view.

2 river: life force; journey; source of food (mahinga kai); a means to travel; home of the taniwha.

3 the waka: transport; that which brought ancestors to Aotearoa; connection to an iwi; carries the mana of the Māori people; means unity (He waka eke noa – we are all in this together).

POEM: *Feelings and Memories of a Kuia* by Apirana Taylor (pages 100–109)

Pre-reading activities (pages 100–101)
PREDICTING

1 a Some suggestions.

Feelings: deeply personal; influenced by own experiences and values; experienced by one person only.

Memories: the past; painful; positive; influenced by time passing; different people can have different memories of the same event.

Kuia: Māori word for elderly woman, grandmother, female elder; someone who has lived a long life; someone who has seen change.

b Answers will vary.

Immediate response (page 103)
These are your personal responses to the work and, as such, we have not listed the answers as there will be many different responses.

Unpacking the text (pages 103–104)
1 **IDENTIFYING THE TONE**

a These answers will depend on the individual but for us: sadness, concern for the present compared to the past. An acknowledgement that when two cultures meet, usually one ends up worse off.

b ii **Positive:** polite; liked to talk; leisurely; got things done; jokes; very happy; lots of fish; plenty; fat juicy pigeon; dinner swam past.

Negative: not Māori anymore; rush; don't look happy; chopped down; river damned; polluted; difficult; war; would have been; killed; overseas; for what; once we had; once we got; lost; unhappy; not know why.

iii *The tone is mostly* reflective and nostalgic *because of* words such as 'once we had' and 'would have been.'

c The main subject is the urbanisation of Māori and how it has come at a cost to their culture.

d One possible answer: 'These Māori today / are not Māori any more … and for what / So we could live in quarter-acre sections'.

e *The writer is* upset about the urbanisation of Māori *because he uses words/phrases like* 'So in the end / we could be lost / and unhappy / and not know why' *when describing* what has happened to the Māori people. *These words make the reader think about* the impact of colonisation on a native people *because* the narrator, the kuia, forces us to see how things were before urbanisation.

Identifying the 'point of change' (page 104–105)
1 First = line 13. Second = line 39.

2 First = the atmosphere in the first stanza is matter-of-fact in a resigned way. That 'These Māori today / are not Māori any more'. Second = the atmosphere before the second change is nostalgic and positive. The poem has strong imagery of a relaxed, friendly and abundant lifestyle, where food was fresh and plentiful and people had time for each other.

3 a 'used to make jokes'

b 'plenty / of fat juicy pigeon'

4 The atmosphere after the second change becomes almost bitter. The words are harsh, 'chopped', 'damned' and 'polluted,' and the rhythm changes. The kuia is accusatory, clearly stating 'the closer / the Pākehā got to us / the more difficult / he made it for us to live'.

Summarise (page 105)
Some suggestions.

1 This poem is about how the urbanisation of the Māori has come at a huge cost to their cultural practices. The narrator, the kuia, believes it was not worth it.

2 *The poet wanted to teach us about* the impact of colonisation/urbanisation of the Māori people *because* he wanted us to think about how a culture has been lost and also how messing with the natural environment has meant that traditional sources of kai (food) have now been changed as well as the desire for these traditional foods which have been replaced by modern, Western ones.

Identifying and discussing the effects of how the poem is communicated (page 105)
1 Personal pronoun: 'I don't know', 'my mokopuna', I think; they cooked us

Parallel structure: 'they were polite / they liked to talk / they walked at a leisurely pace'

Use of te reo Māori: 'mokopuna', 'kuia', 'koro', 'kai', 'ake ake'

Contrast: 'Today my mokopuna always rush / yet never seem to do a thing', 'So we could eat / Hamburgers/ where once we got / fresh kai'

Imagery: 'When I was a girl / we had big gardens', 'plenty / of fat juicy pigeon'

Past tense: 'we went', 'we'd shake', 'there were'

Adjectives: 'plenty', 'fat juicy', 'chopped', 'polluted'

Rhetorical question: 'and for what'

Language focus: Irony (page 107)
Answers will vary; get a friend or teacher to check yours.

1 People should be happy/old people don't know things/modern living is better for everyone/it's a good thing being given a quarter acre.

2 People are not happy/the kuia appreciates and understands what really brings happiness/a quarter acre is not very much land compared with what the people used to own.

3 Suggesting perhaps that the old way of living was better for people/listen to the wisdom of our old people because they can remember a different (and better for most Māori) time.

4 'always rush / yet never seem to do a thing'. This is poking fun at the busyness of our modern lives.

SET 2

PROSE: *Is it hot enough for you yet?* by David Slack (pages 114–120)

Immediate response (pages 115–116)
These are your personal responses to the work and, as such, we have not listed the answers as there will be many different responses.

Post-reading questions (page 116)
1 The world is in bad shape and people are not taking seriously how close we are to destroying the earth. Words like 'deadly' tell us how serious he thinks things are.

2 David Slack was feeling guilty because the situation he was in – the happy situation of a family Christmas – showed up even more what was going on around him. Most of us think of Christmas as a happy time of celebration as we eat well but it can also be a time where people argue about issues like climate change. By using this scenario, Slack is reminding us that often there are underlying problems despite things looking good on the surface.

1 IDENTIFYING THE TONE

b ii Positive: Christmas; special; right direction; readily; truth; sweet; future; better; vastly better; free; sustainable; doable; care.

Negative: scientists are wrong; too small; immolation; hypocrite; worried; climate change; disqualify; argument; falsehoods; inconvenient; risk; gone; give up; fossil fuels; unsustainable; hotter; worse; not be good; awful; horrible; deadly; deadly heat; damn whining.

iii *The tone is mostly* aggressive and confronting *because of words such as* 'hypocrite', 'wrong' and 'worse'.

c Climate change is here and it's bad.

d 'The hotter it gets, the worse things are.'

e *The writer is* anxious about climate change *because he uses words like* 'unsustainable', 'hotter' and 'worse' *when describing* the effects of climate change. *These words make the reader think about* what they are doing to reduce climate change because Slack points out that we can change things if we act now.

Language focus: Questions (including rhetorical) and assertions (page 119)

Here are some suggestions, however answers will vary; get a friend or teacher to check yours.

List of questions:

- Why doesn't China do something?
- Why in the face of undeniable truth, do people still grasp at every other possible argument, up to and including complete falsehoods about greens impeding hazard reductions?
- Is it that the truth is just too inconvenient?
- Is that what the Murdoch media is up to?
- Does he really believe that's acceptable?

List of assertions:

- It's always a special day for climate change bingo.
- Taking a stand on climate change but not doing every last thing you can does not disqualify your position.
- Anything that reduces the harm is a step in the right direction.
- But doing nothing doesn't mean that things will stay as they are.
- That option has gone.
- The hotter it gets; the worse things are. And it will not be good. It will be awful. Horrible. Deadly.
- if nothing changes it will be really, really hot, a whole lot of the time.
- But if we do act, the future can be better. It's vastly better.
- There is so much we can do. It's knowable, it's doable.

POEM: *Me, the Labourer* **by Eti Sa'aga (pages 121–126)**

Immediate response (page 122)

These are your personal responses to the work and, as such, we have not listed the answers as there will be many different responses.

1 IDENTIFYING THE TONE

b ii Positive: sun; comfort; friend; cool on my body; warm my soul; good; pretty.

Negative: sweat; pave the road; stares and frowns; dirty work; think of me; very little money; pretty speeches; rich man; satisfied; race; silently; no one sees me; when is it to be.

iii *The tone is mostly* resentful *because of words such as* 'very little money' and 'The richman rides ahead'.

c The main subject is how the road worker feels unseen/ignored by the rest of society.

d 'No one remembers me / for the road I made.'

e *The writer is* resentful *because he uses words/phrases like* 'very little money' and 'The richman rides ahead' *when describing* the labourer's experiences. *These words make the reader think about* the 'worker' and how they do all the hard work but rarely get acknowledged *because* it points out how the 'richman' gets to take the glory when things are completed.

Identifying the point of change (pages 123)

1 Line 11.

2 Atmosphere is quite calm and nice, 'friend is the wind' and 'sun / is warm my soul'.

3 As above.

4 After the change the atmosphere becomes resentful.

Identifying and discussing the effects of how the poem is communicated (page 124)

1 Personal pronoun: 'Me, / the labourer', 'my body', 'They don't like me'

Imagery: 'sweat / in the sun', 'the wind / is cool on my body'

Cliché: 'to do their dirty work'

Repetition: 'richman', 'have me'; 'think of me', 'No one ...'

Alliteration: 'pave the **r**oad / for the **r**ichman / to **r**ide on'

Personification: 'cars ... race on'

Contrast: 'richman rides ahead ... More cars ... I walk'

Language focus: Diction (page 125)

- 'richman': this mimics the way the narrator says the two words quickly so that they have, for the labourer, become one word.
- 'I does my work hard': The use of the verb 'does' instead of I 'am' or 'I work hard' means a focus on the hard sound 'does' like an emphasis so that he is assuring the reader of how hard he works.
- 'Is good to have me / think of me': Putting the word 'good' second with the repetition of 'me' draws attention to the positive adjective associated with himself. This is to remind the reader that having a positive self-view matters for everyone.
- 'think I'm very good worker': Though the grammar is incorrect, the message is still clear: the simple adverb ('very') plus the positive adjective ('good') emphasise that the labourer knows his value.

 ISBN: 9780170454445